SCHOOL LEADER'S
GUIDE TO

the Common
CORE

*Achieving Results Through **Rigor** and **Relevance***

James A. Bellanca ❧ Robin J. Fogarty
Brian M. Pete ❧ Rebecca L. Stinson

Solution Tree | Press

a division of
Solution Tree

555 North Morton Street
Bloomington, IN 47404
800.733.6786 (toll free) / 812.336.7700
FAX: 812.336.7790
email: info@solution-tree.com
solution-tree.com

Visit **go.solution-tree.com/leadership** to download the reproducibles in this book.

Printed in the United States of America

17 16 15 14 13   2 3 4 5

Library of Congress Cataloging-in-Publication Data

Bellanca, James A., 1937-
   School leader's guide to the common core : achieving results through rigor and relevance / James A. Bellanca, Robin J. Fogarty, Brian M. Pete.
      pages cm
   Includes bibliographical references and index.
   ISBN 978-1-936764-45-7 (perfect bound) 1. Education--Standards--United States. 2. Educational change--United States. 3. School administrators--United States--Handbooks, manuals, etc. 4. School principals--United States--Handbooks, manuals, etc. I. Fogarty, Robin. II. Pete, Brian M. III. Title.
   LB3060.83.B45 2013
   379.1'58--dc23
                              2013016014

Solution Tree
Jeffrey C. Jones, CEO
Edmund M. Ackerman, President

Solution Tree Press
President: Douglas M. Rife
Publisher: Robert D. Clouse
Editorial Director: Lesley Bolton
Managing Production Editor: Caroline Weiss
Senior Production Editor: Joan Irwin
Copy Editor: Sarah Payne-Mills
Proofreader: Elisabeth Abrams
Cover and Text Designer: Rian Anderson

Dedicated to the mindful, innovative, and entrepreneurial students of the 21st century, who are inheriting the legacies of the past and the unknowns of the future.

The lasting measure of good teaching is what the individual student learns and carries away.

—Barbara Harrell Carson

Acknowledgments

At a political level, we acknowledge the developers of the Common Core State Standards (CCSS): the National Governors Association Center for Best Practices (NGA) and the Council of Chief State School Officers (CCSSO). Their vision and execution of rigorous and relevant national standards parallel the skill sets the Partnership for 21st Century Skills (www.p21.org) defines for 21st century citizens.

At a professional level, we extend our gratitude to the dedicated leaders in the state, district, and local arenas for their eager adoption, overwhelming support, and ongoing vigilance of the Common Core State Standards. If done with integrity of implementation and fidelity to the mission, these standards can be a true and challenging game changer for our youth.

At the publishing level, we wholeheartedly thank Solution Tree Press and, particularly, Douglas Rife, Robb Clouse, and Claudia Wheatley for their encouragement to do this book. In addition, of course, we are indebted to the amazing publishing staff of editors, designers, and production staff for bringing this edition to fruition.

Solution Tree Press would like to thank the following reviewers:

Rick Ellingworth
Superintendent of Schools
Redwood Area School District
Redwood Falls, Minnesota

Rosalind LaRocque
Associate Director
American Federation of Teachers, AFL-CIO
Washington, DC

Visit **go.solution-tree.com/leadership** to download the reproducibles in this book.

Table of Contents

Reproducible pages are in italics.

CHAPTER 2
THE SHIFT IN IMPLEMENTATION   **43**
Sustaining Professional Learning

CHAPTER 3
THE SHIFT IN INSTRUCTION   **61**
Attaining Rigor and Real-World Relevance

CHAPTER 4
THE SHIFT IN COACHING AND FEEDBACK   **95**
Leading With Guiding Principles

CHAPTER 5

THE SHIFT IN ASSESSING RESULTS   **121**
Informing All Stakeholders

About the Authors

James A. Bellanca is founder and executive director of the Illinois Consortium for 21st Century Schools (www.ilc21 .org). His extensive experience as a classroom teacher, alternative school director, professional developer, publisher, and intermediate service center consultant has given him a wide scope of school transformation experience. Jim is the author of *Enriched Learning Projects: A Practical Pathway to 21st Century Skills*; the editor, with Ron Brandt, of *21st Century Skills*; coauthor of *How to Teach Thinking Skills Within the Common Core: Seven Key Student Proficiencies of the New National Standards*; editor and contributor to *Connecting the 21st Century Dots*, the Partnership for 21st Century Skills' blog; and writer for his own blog, *PBL Deeper Learning Matters* on the Illinois Consortium's website. He is the designer and lead facilitator for the 21st century skills professional development for school change program MindQuest21.

Robin J. Fogarty is the president of Robin Fogarty & Associates, a Chicago-based, minority-owned educational publishing and consulting company. Her doctorate is in curriculum and human resource development from Loyola University of Chicago. A leading proponent of the thoughtful classroom, Robin has trained educators throughout the world in curriculum, instruction, and assessment strategies. She has taught at all levels, from kindergarten to college, served as an administrator, and consulted with state departments and ministries of education in the United States, Puerto Rico, Russia, Canada, Australia, New Zealand, Germany, Great Britain, Singapore, Korea, and the Netherlands. Robin has published articles in *Educational Leadership*, *Phi Delta Kappan*, and the *Journal of Staff Development*. She is the author of numerous publications, including *Brain-Compatible Classrooms*,

Ten Things New Teachers Need to Succeed, Literacy Matters, How to Integrate the Curricula, Close the Achievement Gap, Informative Assessment: When It's Not About a Grade, Twelve Brain Principles That Make the Difference, and *Nine Best Practices That Make the Difference.* Her recent work includes the two-book leadership series *From Staff Room to Classroom* and the books *Supporting Differentiated Instruction: A Professional Learning Communities Approach* and *How to Teach Thinking Skills Within the Common Core: Seven Key Student Proficiencies of the New National Standards.*

Brian M. Pete is the cofounder of Robin Fogarty & Associates, an educational publishing and consulting company. He comes from a family of educators—college professors, school superintendents, teachers, and teachers of teachers. He has a rich background in professional development. Brian has worked with and videotaped classroom teachers and professional experts in schools throughout the United States, Europe, Asia, Australia, and New Zealand. He has an eye for the "teachable moment" and the words to describe what he sees as skillful teaching. Brian's educational videos include *Best Practices: Classroom Management* and *Best Practices: Active Learning Classrooms.* He is coauthor of many books, which include *Data Driven Decisions, Twelve Brain Principles That Make the Difference, Nine Best Practices That Make the Difference, The Adult Learner, A Look at Transfer,* and *From Staff Room to Classroom I* and *II.* Among recent publications, Brian has coauthored *Supporting Differentiated Instruction: A Professional Learning Communities Approach* and *How to Teach Thinking Skills Within the Common Core: Seven Key Student Proficiencies of the New National Standards.* In addition, Brian is a member of the board for the Illinois Consortium for 21st Century Schools and is a guest blogger on its website.

Rebecca L. Stinson is principal of Claremont Academy Elementary School in the Chicago Public Schools (CPS) system. She was selected to open new public schools in two of Chicago's most underserved and underperforming communities. The CEO of the CPS system recognized Rebecca in the yearly principal evaluations for achieving high student scores in reading and mathematics, which put these schools in the top 7 percent of schools that were accelerating. Claremont Academy's innovative gender-specific classroom structure is featured in the *Phi Delta Kappan* article "Separating the Boys From the Girls" about educating U.S. African American males.

She is a member of the Association for Supervision and Curriculum Development (ASCD) and presented Data! Dialogue! and Decisions! at the 2007 ASCD Conference in Anaheim, California, and Leading Common Core: Knowing the Look-Fors at the 2013 ASCD Conference in Chicago, Illinois. As a member of the Office of Principal Preparation and Development, she served as a mentor for new principals, assisting in training school staff, creating professional development activities, and guiding school improvement planning activities for academic advancement. She is a past vice president of the Jack and Jill of America Chicago Chapter. Rebecca has a bachelor of arts from Howard University in Washington, DC, and a master of education from National Louis University in Chicago.

To book James A. Bellanca, Robin J. Fogarty, Brian M. Pete, or Rebecca L. Stinson for professional development, contact pd@solution-tree.com.

Introduction

Alice Kingsley: This is impossible.
The Hatter: Only if you believe it is.

—Lewis Carroll

The 21st century has brought a new set of challenges into the facilities of the school leader's office. The Common Core State Standards, 21st century skills, common assessments, project-based learning, digital literacy, blended learning, and more have moved the old furniture aside, creating a whole new arrangement of problems to solve. The responsibility for turning these challenges into effective practice, making sure that all students are ready for college and careers in the fast-evolving global economy, falls mostly on the shoulders of the school leadership team, which may include principals, assistant principals, department chairs, or instructional coaches. The job of meeting these challenges may look impossible. However, the challenges call for principals or their leadership delegates to continue doing what they do best: watching out for students and their learning as they support the teachers in their work—the new challenges just involve a new context with some new expectations. The furniture is shifted, but the possibility of new arrangements holds great promise for students' future comforts.

The Common Core State Standards (CCSS) introduce modifications that have ramifications for how schools will function for years to come. The CCSS have six attributes that distinguish them from most previous state standards.

1. The standards are *fewer* in number. The adage "less is more" describes the CCSS. The reduced number of standards provides focus, depth, and coherence across the grades.

2. The standards are *clearly stated*. The CCSS aim for clarity and specificity by delineating expectations in four strands for English language arts (Reading, Writing, Speaking and Listening, and Language) and eight Mathematical Practices.

3. The standards are *more rigorous.* The coherent structure of the CCSS provides a broad-based approach to learning outcomes across the curriculum. The ELA/literacy standards augment the content standards in history and social studies, science, and technical subjects.

4. The standards are *internationally benchmarked.* The CCSS draw on resources from international studies—the *Trends in International Mathematics and Science Study* (TIMSS) and *Progress in International Reading Literacy Study* (PIRLS)—to define standards that are comparable to those in high-performing countries. Additionally, the writing team consulted international models (for example, those from Ireland, Finland, Australia, Singapore, and the United Kingdom).

5. The standards are *research* and *evidence based.* Appendix A of the CCSS ELA/literacy describes research resources that support the key elements of the standards (NGA & CCSSO, 2010c). The CCSS for mathematics derive from "research-based learning progressions detailing what is known today about how students' mathematical knowledge, skill, and understanding develop over time" (NGA & CCSSO, 2010e, p. 4).

6. The standards are *aligned with 21st century skills.* The CCSS are designed to build student capacity in such skill areas as critical thinking, problem solving, communication, and collaboration. This approach is consistent with the principles of the Framework for 21st Century Learning (Partnership for 21st Century Skills, 2011).

These six attributes signal that the CCSS are more effective for ensuring that students are well-prepared to compete in the 21st century's global economy. The CCSS offer the potential for deeper learning for all students. These same characteristics suggest that paying attention to business means principals are guiding faculty to make the site-based modifications that will best help their students. These changes open the doors for school leaders and teachers to put into action those best practices and fast-appearing innovations that well-defined research has already identified as most likely to do the job in 21st century classrooms.

Challenges in Instructional Practice

Practice is the key word that drives the many alternatives for skill and concept development in the Common Core. The CCSS signal a shift from ways of learning and teaching that call for students to *recall* information to ways that spotlight how they *apply* that information to achieve deeper learning. With the information explosion that threatens to overwhelm the 21st century work world, brain and mind researchers forewarn schools and the education community about the need to foster how-to-learn skills so students can filter and transfer the mountains of information they face (Bransford, Brown, & Cocking, 2000; Davidson, 2011; Sousa, 2010).

Simply memorizing multiple algebraic formulas or the lines of *Casey at the Bat* (Thayer, 1997) won't be sufficient. Defining *practice* as a student's transfer of knowledge and application to real-world problem solving, the CCSS lead the response that cries out, "The time is now." Follow the leader. The Common Core sets the pace.

Each of the Common Core State Standards engenders shifts in practice. In order to bring more coherence and focus, to match international benchmarks, to promote 21st century skills, and to draw on evidence-based strategies, these standards spotlight modifications that move the emphases of curriculum, instruction, and assessment in new directions. Significant challenges in both the ELA/literacy and mathematics standards impact daily practice. How well the school leadership guides teachers in making the mental shifts that nudge these paper shifts into real-world practice will be a major determinant in how well the school community works to align itself with best practices for teaching and learning in the 21st century.

Challenges in the CCSS ELA/Literacy

Five challenges enhance the shift in ELA/literacy. First, there is the challenge of shared responsibility for literacy across the disciplines. The second is the challenge of balance in rich literary and informational texts. The third challenge is rigor in content and cognitive skills. The fourth is the challenge for the renewal of instructional emphasis, and lastly, the challenge of relevance in real-world applications. Deeper learning is a natural result of these challenges (Pellegrino & Hilton, 2012).

Shared Responsibility for Literacy Across the Disciplines

The ELA/literacy standards define requirements for English language arts (K–12) and literacy in history and social studies, science, and technical subjects (grades 6–12). In grades K–5, the strands are Reading, Writing, Speaking and Listening, and Language. Two strands—Reading and Writing—set expectations for literacy in subject areas in grades 6–12; these standards are intended to augment, not replace, content standards in those subjects (NGA & CCSSO, 2010a). This emphasis on an *integrated model of literacy* calls on leaders to balance writing, speaking, and listening instruction with the time allocated to reading and to foster these communication skills across all content areas. This instructional model has implications for assessments that the Partnership for Assessment of Readiness for College and Careers (PARCC) and the Smarter Balanced Assessment Consortium (SBAC) are developing to accompany the CCSS. (You should check your state website for the latest information about the progress of the assessment consortia, or visit www.parcconline.org or www.smarterbalanced.org for more information.) These summative assessments will require students to write analyses for narrative and informational text excerpts.

The implication for the curriculum is clear: the Writing strand needs its fair share of attention. As Joelle Brummitt-Yale (2008) notes:

> Indeed, innovative principals will recognize that this call is a window of opportunity. Even if some state education offices place all the summative assessment emphases on reading tests, these principals will recognize what the research says about the reading-writing synergy as a powerful strategy for increasing students' reading abilities.

The synergistic combination of writing and reading instruction provides insight into the potential for achievement gains on high-stakes tests by students collaboratively engaged in project-based learning. This approach to learning provides additional data about students' speaking and listening performances.

Balance in Rich Literary and Informational Texts

The Reading strand has two parts: Standards for Literature and Standards for Informational Text across all grades. This perspective requires elementary school teachers to devote at least 50 percent, middle school teachers to devote at least 55 percent, and high school teachers to devote at least 70 percent of readers' time to informational text. For many elementary and middle school teachers, this expectation will mean much more than purchasing digital books for the library. It also means teachers will have to shunt aside some of the old literature favorites, making room for nonfiction texts in greater abundance.

In high school, English teachers may carry a lesser burden for this balance. Student reading in other disciplines—mathematics, science, social studies, and technology—contributes to the 70 percent informational text goal. English teachers will need to subtract less time from the current schedule for reading literature texts, writing, speaking, and listening and may even benefit from the inclusion of some informational text. With the shift to a *shared* responsibility for expanding the study of informational text, schools will be responding to the Common Core's agenda to develop students' discipline-based informational text reading skills concurrently with expansion of their knowledge of recent developments in each discipline. In this way, schools will also be closer to achieving the NGA and CCSSO expectation for students' increased readiness for college and career in a global economy.

Rigor in Content and Cognitive Skills

The third challenge involves an intentional, grade-level increase in text complexity: "a grade-by-grade 'staircase' of increasing complexity that rises from beginning reading to the college and career readiness level" (NGA & CCSSO, 2010b, p. 8). The CCSS define three factors to assist teachers in knowing how to assess the difficulty of texts they use with their students: (1) *quantitative measures*, such as readability formulae; (2) *qualitative factors*, such as levels of meaning, structure, and knowledge demands; and (3) *reader and task considerations*, such as motivation and experience (NGA & CCSSO, 2010c).

To ensure the smoothest climb up the staircase of text complexity and to strengthen each student's chance for reading success, teachers can compile month-to-month data that students can carry on to the next grades. Such data will help most if they identify students' progress on aspects of text complexity—levels of meaning and structure, language conventionality and clarity, and knowledge—rather than record the books read or grades on recall tests.

Consistent with the emphasis on text complexity, the CCSS increase the focus on cognitive development by highlighting explicit thinking skills that thread through the standards. State standards tend to focus on detailed curriculum content and overemphasize test-preparation activity. In most states, the mandated, standards-aligned annual tests at the elementary grades check students' acquired knowledge at the recall level. Yet, from the times of Plato and Confucius, critical thinking and creative thinking have driven rich teaching and learning experiences. In the 21st century, seismic forces are driving schools worldwide to push these cognitive skills to the forefront. In addition to pressures from global corporations in search of employees sharp with these skills, international tests such as the Programme for International Student Assessment (PISA; Organisation for Economic Co-operation and Development [OECD], 2009) have drawn attention to the average and below-average performance of U.S. students as thinkers and problem solvers in reading, mathematics, and science. That angst was a major impetus for creating the Common Core State Standards as a national priority.

Renewal of Instructional Emphasis

The ELA/literacy standards focus on developing students' ability to read and understand complex texts. This expectation means that teachers must modify their practice to enable students to delve deeply into texts rather than simply having them make personal connections to the stories. Many teachers, notably at the elementary level, are accustomed to using basal texts and narratives selected to spark student interest. For example, *The Little Engine That Could*, *Cinderella*, *Curious George*, *Madeline*, *Sarah, Plain and Tall*, *Charlotte's Web*, and the *Harry Potter* series provide role models for students to emulate. As students discuss the characters in these popular narratives, teachers have helped them connect the stories to their daily lives, most often by asking students how they feel about what is happening to their favorite character. Secondary content-area teachers who have little or no preparation in teaching strategies for reading informational text will face the greatest challenge. Not only will they need skill development for this task but they will have to find ways to fit the instruction into an already crowded schedule.

The CCSS require teachers to move the focus of instruction to reading closely to determine key ideas and details, to understand the author's craft and text structure, and to integrate and evaluate ideas (NGA & CCSSO, 2010b). The shift asks teachers to elicit students' understanding of the authors' intent and how they craft an engaging and meaningful story or informational essay. Through explicit instruction, teachers provide models for students' independent reading of complex texts.

When it comes time for assessment, teachers will need to examine how skillfully students make close-text analyses about what authors suggest; how well they analyze story parts, such as character, tone, setting, and theme, that relate to the whole story; how thoroughly they understand what is implied by word choice and syntax; and how they relate facts and details to ideas or arguments in nonfiction text. Teachers will do this in the context of computerized assessments, such as the PARCC and SBAC assessments (see page 127), that ask the students to put their analyses into coherent and well-formulated paragraphs.

Relevance in Real-World Applications

The Common Core State Standards place an increased emphasis on deep comprehension, mathematical problem solving, and cross-curricular literacy and problem-solving skills as intentional *do* outcomes for all students to be college and career ready. The challenge will be to move from the skill-and-drill regime that permeates the instructional arena and make way for meaningful project-based learning, problem-based scenarios, and robust performance-based exercises that require authentic application of the academic knowledge to the real world. This challenge offers a welcome opportunity for real and significant change in schooling: change that stresses the practical use of literacy strategies and mathematical skills and concepts in place of fostering inert knowledge for students. James Pellegrino and Margaret Hilton (2012) synthesize those best practices that lead to the deeper learning that researchers mark as essential for learning in a global society. These practices call for instruction that fosters critical thinking, shared learning, and evidence-based argumentation in a "positive learning community in which students gain content knowledge and also develop intrapersonal and interpersonal competencies" (Pellegrino & Hilton, 2012, p. 7).

Challenges in the CCSS Mathematics

The mathematics standards present five challenges that forecast a significant impact on mathematics instruction and assessment. The first challenge focuses on developing proficiency in the Mathematical Practices. The second challenge describes the necessity of concept-rich mathematics to enable students to develop deep understanding of essential mathematical ideas. Problem posing and problem solving, the third challenge, are central to achieving increased rigor in mathematics instruction. The fourth challenge defines the skills—practices in computation and operations—mathematics that ensure mathematical excellence and provide the prerequisites for success in higher mathematics and in real-world applications. Preparation through coaching and feedback, the fifth challenge, explores the potential changes in the teacher's role stemming from the availability of digital resources that students can use in the classroom or at home.

Although the mathematics standards parallel the ELA/literacy standards in the desired results (for example, independence and strong content knowledge), these challenges are meant to spotlight mathematics problem solving as the ultimate goal in each grade. All five interrelated challenges highlight the new emphasis on *practice* in which students are expected to show increased proficiency as critical thinkers and problem solvers, putting the deep understanding of concepts into the practice of solving rigorous real-world problems. No longer will problem solving take a backseat if educators address each challenge.

Proficiency in the Mathematical Practices

The Standards for Mathematical Practice define eight habits of mind or mathematical dispositions that frame K–12 instruction (NGA & CCSSO, 2010e). The Mathematical Practices accompany an overview of mathematics content presented at the beginning of each grade-level section of the CCSS for mathematics. This structure provides a routine reminder of the importance of the expertise that students are expected to attain as they learn mathematics. The listing specifies habits of mind, dispositions, attitudes, and behaviors that are desired outcomes of understanding mathematics content. The eight principles include such cognitive functions as perseverance in solving problems, reasoning abstractly and quantitatively, and communicating precisely. We fully explain the Mathematical Practices in chapter 1 (page 20).

Practices in Concept-Rich Mathematics

The CCSS focus mathematics instruction in a conceptual frame that provides students with deep understanding of core mathematical concepts. This focus on tightly defined problem solving derives from skillful use of reasoning abilities. Students need time to build concepts that will allow them to advance. For instance, *part* and *whole* are relative terms; *ratio* is the relationship between numbers, not the numbers themselves; and *distributive*, *associative*, and *commutative processes* apply to all additions and multiplications of rational numbers. These are difficult concepts that middle-grade students need to fully understand prior to launching into complex problem-solving practices. As students grasp these concepts, they ready themselves to create an increased number of applications that will strengthen their ability to form strong generalizations that are the gist of each mathematics concept they will study in the following years.

The CCSS make clear the value of this challenge of concept-rich mathematics. From kindergarten when students are asked to represent data for the first time until the upper grades when they are asked to use sophisticated tools for statistical analysis, students are challenged to abandon preconceptions and misconceptions that block their understanding of essential mathematical ideas (Ben-Hur, 2006).

Most of these errors spring from mistakes in ways students think about a mathematical concept. In the early grades, it is important that teachers vigorously tackle erroneous preconceptions such as *there is no number smaller than zero.* Teachers cannot give students a set of steps to memorize their way out of this false understanding. Instead, they must assess whether the students have understood the concept and guide them to achieve understanding. To change the students' mindset, the teacher needs to ask students how they came up with an idea, to clarify what does not make sense, and to explain why the answer doesn't make sense. The teacher can then guide the students to grasp the logical view and listen as they explain what and how the new view is related to a new understanding. In other words, as the NGA and CCSSO (2010e) state, "Mathematical understanding and procedural skill are equally important, and both are assessable using mathematical tasks of sufficient richness" (p. 4).

Problem Posing and Problem Solving

Enabling students to apply mathematical understandings to open-ended problems through the formation of problems and alternative solutions in real-world situations is a primary goal of the CCSS. The increased rigor in mathematics instruction places problem solving in a front-row seat instead of in the coat closet. Textbook-bound and assessment-driven instruction has promoted replicated lessons that provide students with step-by-step recipes for completing numerical operations and, time permitting, places problem solving after students finish their worksheets. In addition, the overly fast pace needed to cover the multitude of topics and worksheet pages allows teachers little time to correct misconceptions and build readiness for problem solving in practice. Consequently, as early elementary students advance into more complex concepts, they lack the cognitive foundation for reasoning and problem solving that becomes more essential each year (Ben-Hur, 2006).

Ongoing international assessments and advocacy for 21st century skills keep attention centered on problem solving. For example, OECD (2010b) makes clear its intent to administer tests that focus less on the traditional list of steps used in problem solving—identify the problem, define the problem, and so on—and place greater emphasis on the creative- and critical-thinking skills involved in solving a problem. Thus, the tests will examine how students generate ideas, pose and form the problem, make associations, hypothesize, and infer. These tasks require students to use the creative right side of the brain. To examine the use of the critical left side, the tests will spotlight the quality of reasoning through the analyses, differentiations, and comparisons students use in forming the problem itself and in generating solutions.

Mathematics Computation and Operations

The Standards for Mathematical Content address computation, calculations, and operations in numeracy; functions; measurement; data; algebra; geometry; and statistics and probability (NGA & CCSSO, 2010e). These are the very skills that accompany mathematical excellence and provide the prerequisites for success in higher mathematics and in real-world applications. These are the foundational skills required for learning in the fields of science, mathematics, engineering, and technology.

The CCSS focus explicitly on mathematical literacy employing conceptual reasoning and problem solving. Importantly, the standards also highlight procedures and operations that require student initiative, perseverance, and persistence. These include opportunities for students to reflect on their learning and to converse with others about how they learn mathematics and solve problems, as well as which strategies work the best. Additionally, students must also demonstrate the abilities to compute confidently, calculate with accuracy, and understand the reasonableness of their answer with various strategies that help them confirm their findings.

Preparation Through Coaching and Feedback

As digital technologies make available new tools and programs that students can use at home or in the classroom to help sharpen mathematical reasoning and develop deeper understanding of concepts, a shift in thinking about the role of the teacher in mathematics instruction can occur. The teacher's role is likely to change from *giver of information* to *facilitator of learning* through appropriate and timely coaching and feedback. Websites such as the Khan Academy (www.khanacademy.org; see also TED, 2011), QR Stuff (www.qrstuff.com), or PhET (http://phet.colorado .edu) allow teachers to blend instruction by sending students to online resources that can enrich their interest and proficiency in mathematics. For instance, teachers can *flip* their roles, known as *flip learning*, so students come to the classroom ready for guided practice that enriches understanding gained from the Khan Academy (TED, 2011). Or they can spend in-class time with a challenging science application from PhET, where the teacher's coaching abilities can be best utilized to help students put mathematics skills into science practice. Sites such as Illuminations (http://illuminations.nctm.org) provide vetted activities, strategies, and resources that teachers can build into project-based learning units or adapt as practice sessions. These online tools allow teachers to serve as facilitators and mentors and engage students in understanding standards-aligned concepts, solving problems, and practicing procedures.

About This Book

Meeting the CCSS challenges requires school leaders to engage in a balancing act: one that combines effective instruction and innovative practices. *School Leader's Guide to the Common Core: Achieving Results Through Rigor and Relevance* expands the theme of balance. We aim to show that the Hatter was right to take on what is possible in a time of turmoil and change. Building on evidence of effective instructional leadership, the five chapters delineate ways that leaders can successfully bring innovative practices into a school as they initiate, implement, and institutionalize the Common Core State Standards into the curriculum, instruction, and assessments. Leaders just have to believe! We want to provide guidance to support that commitment. We believe that anyone with a leadership responsibility—principal, assistant principal, department chair, coach, mentor, or instructional supervisor—can benefit from this book. We include a range of examples that are applicable across the K–12 spectrum. These examples are fictionalized accounts of our personal experiences with leaders and teachers.

The layout of the book is simple and straightforward. This introduction leads the way to the more in-depth information presented in the five chapters. Each chapter discusses what we ascertain to be key features of the Common Core State Standards from the school leader's perspective. The writing is conversational in tone and practical by nature with a clear intention of leaving the reader with ideas to share among colleagues and to introduce to the staff in collaborative team meetings. Each chapter ends with three features designed to foster reflection and conversation.

1. **Looking Back:** These chapter summaries invite you to think back to quotations or scenarios that illustrate important themes developed in the chapter and to elaborate on those resources in terms of your own experience.

2. **Discussion Questions:** These guiding questions provide opportunities for reflection and discussion in collaborative faculty, grade-level, or department meetings.

3. **Takeaways:** These main ideas invite you to identify significant topics of particular relevance to your leadership responsibilities and actions.

In addition, online-only reproducibles are available for selected resources in the text (visit **go.solution-tree.com/leadership**), and other reproducibles are included at the end of selected chapters.

Chapter 1: The Shift to the Common Core—Transitioning or Transforming Your School

The shift to the Common Core requires an instructional transition from recall to reasoning and real-world relevance. Chapter 1 begins with the essential question leaders ask themselves, "How might I steer this transition process with efficiency and effectiveness for the desired results?" In response to that provocative question, the chapter delineates the foundational questions that logically follow: What are the Common Core State Standards? Why are the CCSS important? How will schools embrace the CCSS? This chapter provides the broad brush strokes on the CCSS painting, from organizational changes to substantive curricular changes that lead to improved instructional balance between process skills and conceptual content. This chapter sets in place the *whys* of the CCSS that emerge in vivid detail in the subsequent chapters.

Chapter 2: The Shift in Implementation—Sustaining Professional Learning

Leading and learning together are the lessons that drive this chapter on implementation through professional learning support. The chapter opens with a discussion of modeling the relevant content and employing strategies that are the *look-fors* leaders want to see in the classroom. Every time school leaders are in front of the faculty, a grade-level team, a core middle-level team, or a department team, they have opportunities to model instructional excellence. Presenting the information in an engaging and interactive way exemplifies the adage "Actions speak louder than words."

Moving along the implementation pathway, we present a robust discussion of best practices in professional development and the proven elements of design for long-lasting transfer. The conversation fully unpacks the necessity for ongoing support through an informative and interesting look at the important roles of collaborative teams in a professional learning community (PLC). The chapter offers information about supporting teachers to ensure that professional learning becomes an integral and continuous part of the learning organization.

Chapter 3: The Shift in Instruction—Attaining Rigor and Real-World Relevance

The balance in the CCSS between rich, rigorous content and relevant real-world thinking processes raises the bar for college and career readiness for all K–12 students. It's a tall order for some faculty members, as they struggle to align their thinking, practices, and resources to meet the expectations of the CCSS. Discussions in this chapter spotlight four pedagogically sound models of instruction: (1) explicit instruction of thinking skills, (2) close reading of text, (3) concept-rich mathematics instruction, and (4) inquiry learning. These four models exemplify the kinds of instructional excellence needed to raise literacy and mathematical levels and the critical-thinking proficiencies of *all* students—in elementary, middle, and high schools; in rural, urban, and suburban districts; in schools of poverty; and in schools of plenty. Successful implementation of the Common Core ELA/literacy and mathematics standards comes down to the instructional excellence of the teacher in each classroom.

Chapter 4: The Shift in Coaching and Feedback—Leading With Guiding Principles

Coaching and providing feedback are the new skills required of principals and other supervisory administrators for successful implementation of the CCSS. School leaders must coach professional teachers and facilitate learning. For example, we know of a large urban school district that had continued low student achievement but high teacher evaluation ratings. The leaders began to explore why these two complementary elements seemed so out of sync. In interview after interview with practicing principals, the leaders received similar comments about the teacher evaluation check-off form. A sample response was, "If a teacher shows evidence of the behavior, we have to check it off. So, in some cases, the teacher evaluations are somewhat inflated, yet the hardest part of our job is giving constructive feedback to teachers to move along the path of professional expertise." The principals wanted to know, "How do you help a good teacher become a great one?"

This chapter provides examples of the coaching conversations that principals and supervisory administrators have with teachers to accomplish the goal of improving and enhancing teaching expertise. The chapter draws on five school leader principles to paint a picture of the roles of the leader as coach and mentor. We describe four different coaching conversations with a fifth-grade reading teacher, a second-grade reading teacher, an eighth-grade mathematics teacher, and a ninth-grade biology teacher. These scenarios illustrate the care, courage, and commitment of an extraordinary instructional leader.

Chapter 5: The Shift in Assessing Results—Informing All Stakeholders

Assessment plays a crucial role in the implementation of the CCSS. The true mission of the assessments is using the data to inform all stakeholders of students' learning progress. In this chapter, we use the metaphor "Driving Miss Data" to examine the actions necessary to using assessment data well. Many forms of assessment guide the instructional decisions that are best for each particular student. Data are available from a variety of sources—summative assessments, formative assessments, and talks with teachers, students, and parents. Quantitative data at the international, national, state, and local levels provide formalized and publicized grades and rankings that may be necessary for demographic information for comparisons and competitive educational improvements and innovations. However, the key consideration in examining assessment results is this: *the student is at the center of the assessment cycle.*

The discussion in this final chapter flows from rubrics to reports to results. It provides a guide to school leaders about what data are best to collect, how that data might be used to help support student proficiencies in the Common Core, and when the data, testing, and assessing are taking over the mission of preparing college- and career-ready students to face a global community of unknown challenges. School leaders are the gatekeepers of this assessment process, and they set the tone and tenor that permeate collaborative conversations about it.

CHAPTER 1

The Shift to the Common Core

Transitioning or Transforming Your School

Innovation is fostered by information gathered from new connections; from insights gained by journeys into other disciplines or places; from active, collegial networks and fluid, open boundaries. Innovation arises from ongoing circles of exchange, where information is not just accumulated or stored, but created. Knowledge is generated anew from connections that weren't there before.

—Margaret J. Wheatley

"What are you doing out there, Leonardo?" the young boy asked.

"I'm searching for answers to things I do not understand," da Vinci answered.

"That doesn't make any sense."

"True, but it may. It is very important that I ask," the inventor responded. "When I asked why a bird sustains itself in the air, I engineered a way to fly; when I investigated the mystery of the circles a stone makes when dropped in a pond, I comprehended force; when I questioned why thunder is slower and lasts longer than lightning, I understood the speed of sound. My life has been given to asking important questions and finding deeper meaning in the answers."

Leonardo da Vinci is the quintessential model of the innovative thinker. He constantly searched for answers to troubling problems, always turning what he discovered into new knowledge that hadn't been there before. His discoveries had a practical bent as he conceived of new and sustainable tools, products, and ways of working. His plethora of inventions—the parachute, armored car, helicopter, robots, double-hulled boats, single-span bridges, and the viola organista—show his range of creative powers that allowed others to accomplish tasks they previously could not complete.

Leaders Drive Innovation

So what do da Vinci and his innovative thinking have to do with the 21st century principal who is faced with answering the question, How do I help the teachers in this school integrate this newly mandated change for Common Core State Standards for English language arts / literacy and mathematics into daily practice? Da Vinci provides a model, perhaps not just for *managing* operations in a 21st century school, but for solving difficult problems that are required when *leading* a highly effective school and confronting a tsunami of day-to-day challenges—mandates, conflicts, crises, dilemmas, and predicaments including dealing with the kid who missed the school bus. More than ever, the 21st century brings a multitude of willy-nilly daily snags and glitches that threaten to obstruct any attempts to prepare students for their lives in a global, technology-heavy society. In short, the actions of the great inventor who painted the smiling *Mona Lisa* provide the clues to the mindset that separates the 21st century's strongest school leaders from others who inadvertently become mired in minutiae.

Many imagine innovative thinkers as persons like the big inventors who transformed the world by creating the assembly line (Henry Ford and Ransom Olds), by curing diseases (Marie Curie and Patricia Bath), by flying (the Wright Brothers), or by improving revolutionary communication tools (Alexander Graham Bell and Tim Berners-Lee). A different definition of innovator suggests a richer interpretation highly applicable to the 21st century school leader: one who produces practical solutions to existing problems that others can implement to improve the quality of their work and their lives.

Innovation is a preeminent attribute of 21st century school leaders. What other qualities that drive innovation should we look for in these leaders? Figure 1.1 provides some guidance for identifying innovative leadership qualities. The questionnaire asks the school leader to rate himself or herself on such skills as problem analysis, decision making, ability to get others involved in solving problems, and sensitivity to others' problems. Open-ended questions ask for amplification of these attributes, all pointing to the heavy value placed on the school leader as a problem solver.

Another example of leadership qualities is taken from the responses of an informal phone survey in which Jim Bellanca asks twenty principals to identify those characteristics that best define the 21st century principal. The characteristic "problem solver" received the highest rating. One principal reports, "It's a problem a minute. If I don't have to find the solution, teacher teams do the work with me." Another respondent notes, "The day is a sequence of problems to solve. One minute, it's an angry parent. The next, two students start the day with a fight. Then come the bigger things: the latest mandate from the feds, a planning committee to critique teachers' project planning, or an individualized education program [IEP] meeting. It's constantly making lemonade from lemons, so I can be free to do the important stuff—planning how to get our kids ready for their next year's schooling, college, and careers in the fastest-changing world ever. If I don't have a mindset for solving problems—and that

Name: _____ Date: _____

Rank your qualities on a scale of zero (lowest) to five (highest).

Leadership Qualities	Rating Scale
1. Delegating	0 1 2 3 4 5
2. Facilitating collaborative teams	0 1 2 3 4 5
3. Communicating the school mission	0 1 2 3 4 5
4. Making big-picture plans	0 1 2 3 4 5
5. Solving problems	0 1 2 3 4 5
6. Evaluating teacher performance	0 1 2 3 4 5
7. Sharing knowledge of Common Core State Standards	0 1 2 3 4 5
8. Thinking outside the box	0 1 2 3 4 5
My three strongest qualities in order are: 1. 2. 3.	

Figure 1.1: A self-assessment of leadership qualities.

Visit go.solution-tree.com/leadership for a reproducible version of this figure.

means helping others solve problems—I shouldn't be principal . . . and by the way, tomorrow there's a blizzard predicted."

Mandates command a lot of a principal's time and attention. Some come from the central office; others come from the state department of education or the federal department of education. Through whatever channel, these mandates tell the principal the wind never stops blowing. Keep your problem-solving hat on tight, because it is you who will have to figure out how to implement the newest change of direction. In the case of the CCSS, the change portends lots of work, lots of creative thinking, and undoubtedly lots of new challenges.

What Is the Driving Question for School Leaders?

By shifting the implementation of the CCSS from a mandate to a creative challenge, principals can construct a collaborative approach. By creating a driving question that engages their faculties in a problem-solving process, principals are more likely to garner support not only for the planning process but for a full commitment to implement a plan that focuses on teaching for effective learning.

When principals ask successful guiding questions, they will take a faculty immediately into the heart of the matter. Such a question as, What features of our best practice can we retain with the least amount of disruption as we implement the CCSS?

Following exploration of the primary driving question, teachers should answer three additional *clarifying* questions. In this fashion, the driving question guides the entire inquiry process from start to finish. The driving question will remain as the roadside mile marker against which the school team can measure progress. At any time in the planning and implementation processes that a check is needed, the team will answer "How does this help us answer the driving question?" to push the process forward. By referring to the given exemplar and developing their own support questions as markers, principals can guide their teachers forward.

First, the school team needs to ask and answer a *what* question such as, "*What* are the Common Core State Standards?" The team members do this so they can build a simple, precise, and shared language with common understandings. This common vocabulary will ease subsequent discussions. In the unlikely condition that there is no one on the staff with knowledge of these terms, the principal can refer all to the Common Core website (www.corestandards.org) and conduct a guided tour.

Second, the team will ask a *why* question such as, "*Why* are the CCSS important?" The answers to this question will not only deepen the faculty's understanding of the standards but also lay the groundwork to answer the *why* that parents, community members, and students are likely to pose.

Third, the team will turn to the most important question: "*How* will our school embrace the CCSS?" This question will help most when it is specific to classroom practice. Its answers are most important for teachers and students in determining the impact on what happens each day in the classroom. With that *how* comes the criteria that keep teachers' responses simple without complicating their teaching load.

By developing their own criteria, teachers avoid making light of what they are asked to do by reacting superficially with "this too will pass" comments. If principals form teachers into collaborative teams, organized within the school's professional learning community with commitment to a shared goal, they will lighten the burden for all. By adopting a common framework for implementing the CCSS, these collaborative teams have a friendly tool to guide them (see the reproducible "A Common Core Planning Framework" on page 39 and online at **go.solution-tree .com/leadership**).

The framework can be adapted to fit different situations. For example, instead of the school's driving question, the collaborative team may opt to consider any topic in the book including creating a focus for the school's professional learning community.

What Are the Common Core State Standards?

The first support question, "What are the Common Core State Standards?" leads to two answers: one short and one long. The *short* answer is this: These are a U.S. set of K–12 standards in English language arts / literacy and mathematics. These standards are meant to guide school leaders and teachers in revising their curriculum, instruction, and assessment to align and adopting state priorities for what all students need to know and do for living, learning, and working in the 21st century's global economy. The introduction and the layout of the Common Core provide an organized structure and well-defined reference for the English language arts / literacy and mathematics standards (NGA & CCSSO, 2010a).

The *long* answer requires a more detailed look. This long look highlights the classroom applications that teachers are going to make for their CCSS-based instruction and assessment. The long look does not require teachers to become PhD candidates completing in-depth research on the total standards packet. Nor does it require that all teachers study the total K–12 package or spend time unpacking individual standards in each strand to make a matrix that shows the relationships among the standards. That's been done already (for example, see www.parcconline.org /CommonCoreImplementationRubricTool). In addition, the official CCSS website provides a handy reference that teachers can use regularly to clarify their ideas.

All approaches that have teachers listening to lectures about the standards or memorizing terms may suit academic study but have little to do with preparing teachers to skillfully apply the standards as guides to a more rigorous, relevant, and results-directed curriculum that prepares students to function day to day in the 21st century global economy. Instead, what teachers do need is an innovative principal to focus each grade-level team on how the standards play out for the grade and how they build on one another across grade levels. From this approach, the teachers will gain a practical working understanding of the parts in relationship to the whole.

The long answer that pertains to teachers' understanding of what these standards are will come most readily from a shared inquiry of the CCSS. Some states and districts have prepared their own sites, and we recommend that teachers and principals in those situations examine those resources.

One summer institute day or two half-day study sessions will suffice for elementary grade-level teams to lay the groundwork for understanding their grade's mathematics and English language arts standards. Middle-grade teachers, including science, technology, and social studies specialists, can concentrate on the grades 6–8 English language arts and literacy standards in their subject areas. Secondary teachers can work in their departments or in cross-disciplinary grade-level teams. In all sessions, principals can make the most beneficial use of time by engaging teachers in application study of the standards so that each participant leaves with practical takeaways to use the next day.

Organization of the ELA/Literacy Standards

Being familiar with the structure and language of the CCSS ensures that collaborative team members share common vocabulary that facilitates communication. In this book, we've used a simplified version of the *dot notation system* to identify the standards. Additionally, the CCSS use URIs (uniform resource identifiers) and GUIDs (globally unique identifiers) to locate each standard in databases and computer systems. The dot notation system is the preferred number system for educators when referring to the CCSS in conversations. Visit www.corestandards.org/common -core-state-standards-official-identifiers-and-xml-representation for more information. (Visit **go.solution-tree.com/leadership** to access the links in this book.)

Figure 1.2 defines the different elements of the Common Core State Standards for English language arts / literacy. Grade-specific standards parallel the anchor standards for college and career readiness. Figure 1.2 shows one anchor standard for Reading, the domain Key Ideas and Details, and standards for grade 1 students.

Additionally, the ELA standards can be compared to a skeleton. Think of the *strand* as the backbone or spine, *anchor standards* as the major limbs, *domains* as the hands and feet, and the *standards* as the fingers and toes. Every grade has the same skeleton, but it becomes more mature each year. Visit **go.solution-tree.com /leadership** for the reproducible "Figurative Representation of Reading Strand," which illustrates the Reading strand domains that apply to both literature and informational text.

Organization of the Mathematics Standards

The organization of the mathematics standards differs from that of the ELA/literacy standards. The mathematics standards feature two components: (1) Standards for Mathematical Practice and (2) Standards for Mathematical Content (NGA & CCSSO, 2010e). The Standards for Mathematical Practice define areas of expertise—habits of mind—students need to develop to understand and use mathematics effectively. The eight Mathematical Practices are the following (see also NGA & CCSSO, 2010e, pp. 6–8).

- **Mathematical Practice 1:** Make sense of problems and persevere in solving them.
- **Mathematical Practice 2:** Reason abstractly and quantitatively.
- **Mathematical Practice 3:** Construct viable arguments and critique the reasoning of others.

ELA/literacy standards are organized in three main sections: (1) K–5 ELA, (2) grades 6–12 ELA, and (3) grades 6–12 literacy in history and social studies, science, and technical subjects. Three appendices accompany the main document: (1) "Appendix A: Research Supporting Key Elements of the Standards," (2) "Appendix B: Text Exemplars and Sample Performance Tasks," and (3) "Appendix C: Samples of Student Writing."

Strands are the components in each section for K–5 and 6–12: Reading, Writing, Speaking and Listening, and Language. The Reading strand has two parts: Reading Standards for Literature and Reading Standards for Informational Text. In K–5, the Reading strand has a third part: Foundational Skills. The literacy standards focus on two strands: Reading and Writing.

Anchor standards define expectations for college and career readiness (CCRA). They define general, cross-disciplinary expectations for each strand: Reading, Writing, Speaking and Listening, and Language. The anchor standards are numbered consecutively for each strand. For example, CCSS.ELA-Literacy.CCRA.R.1 signifies college and career readiness anchor standard (CCRA), reading strand (R), anchor standard one (1). The Reading and Writing strands for literacy in history / social studies, science, and technical subjects have anchor standards. For example, CCSS.ELA-Literacy.WHST.9–10.4 signifies writing strand (W), history (H), science (S), technical subjects (T), grade band (9–10), anchor standard four (4).

Domains define categories of anchor standards for each of the ELA strands. The domains are consistent across all the grades and ensure continuity as the standards increase in rigor and complexity. The four domains in the Reading strand are (1) Key Ideas and Details, (2) Craft and Structure, (3) Integration of Knowledge and Ideas, and (4) Range of Reading and Level of Text Complexity.

Grade-specific standards define what students should understand and be able to do at the end of the year. These standards correspond to the anchor standard with the same designation. For example, CCSS.ELA-Literacy.RL.6.1 signifies Reading Standards for Literature (RL), grade 6 (6), and standard one (1) in the domain Key Ideas and Details.

Grade bands are skills progressions by grade levels—K–2, 3–5, 6–8, 9–10, and 11–12.

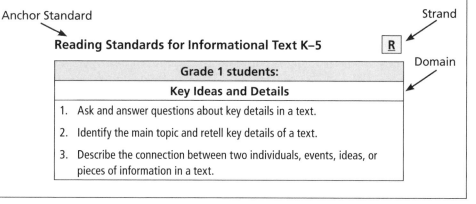

Figure 1.2: How to read the CCSS ELA/literacy.

Source: Adapted from NGA & CCSSO, 2010b, pp. 13, 20, and 66.

*Visit **go.solution-tree.com/leadership** for a reproducible version of this figure.*

- **Mathematical Practice 4:** Model with mathematics.
- **Mathematical Practice 5:** Use appropriate tools strategically.
- **Mathematical Practice 6:** Attend to precision.
- **Mathematical Practice 7:** Look for and make use of structure.
- **Mathematical Practice 8:** Look for and express regularity in repeated reasoning.

These practices describe ways students should engage with mathematical content as they progress throughout the elementary, middle, and high school years. The Standards for Mathematical Content define the topics to be studied in grades K–12. At each grade level, teachers are asked to develop the content by helping students connect practice with content. In this way, students will become proficient in applying the Mathematical Practices and developing their ability to understand mathematics and apply that understanding in new situations.

The Standards for Mathematical Content contain material familiar to mathematics teachers although the sequence of topics may not be consistent with their previous experience with mathematics curriculum. Table 1.1 summarizes the CCSS mathematics content across K–8. The table shows the progression of mathematics topics beginning with the domain Counting and Cardinality, which applies to kindergarten only. Geometry appears at all grade levels (see table 3.3, page 80, for a description of the Geometry domain clusters), and new domains are introduced at later grade levels, such as Statistics and Probability in grade 6 and Functions in grade 8. The high school mathematics standards are organized in six conceptual categories, one of which is Geometry.

The Mathematical Practices are integral to instruction of mathematical content. For instance, the word *understand* in any mathematics standard signals teachers to help students connect mathematics knowledge, often procedural, to the practical *how to*. Students learning mathematics with the CCSS will be expected to demonstrate their proficiency in using the Mathematical Practices. This is an important shift from situations in which students could memorize procedures. NGA and CCSSO, developers of the mathematics standards, maintain that making sense of mathematics is a balanced combination of content and practice. They note, "These standards are not intended to be new names for old ways of doing business. They are a call to take the next step" (NGA & CCSSO, 2010e, p. 5). More than anything else, to support the implementation of the CCSS, mathematics teachers can develop their own understanding of the eight Mathematical Practices by tying their prior knowledge of mathematics content (for example, "What is a fraction?") to these practices. The designated change leader can facilitate teachers' most dramatic, standards-aligned improvement by encouraging in-depth team study that produces new lessons that combine the Mathematical Practices and the mathematics curriculum. Posting the

Table 1.1: CCSS for Mathematics Domains Across Grades K–8

Mathematics Domain	Kinder-garten	Grade 1	Grade 2	Grade 3	Grade 4	Grade 5	Grade 6	Grade 7	Grade 8
Counting and Cardinality	X								
Operations and Algebraic Thinking	X	X	X	X	X	X			
Number and Operations in Base Ten	X	X	X	X	X	X			
Measurement and Data	X	X	X	X	X	X			
Geometry	X	X	X	X	X	X	X	X	X
Number and Operations—Fractions				X	X	X			
Ratios and Proportional Relationships							X	X	
The Number System							X	X	X
Expressions and Equations							X	X	X
Statistics and Probability							X	X	X
Functions									X
The Number System							X	X	X

Source: Adapted from NGA & CCSSO, 2010e.

*Visit **go.solution-tree.com/leadership** for a reproducible version of this table.*

Standards for Mathematical Practice in every classroom and using the list to guide professional development activities provide teachers with frequent opportunities to review the practices and think about how to incorporate them in lessons (see the reproducible "Standards for Mathematical Practice" on page 40). These activities focus on responding to the essential question, How do we modify our mathematics curriculum in order to refocus our students' study so that it is balanced with process and content? Principals can provide reminders of what is essential in understanding the CCSS for mathematics. To ensure teachers are focused and consistent in preparing students for college and careers in the 21st century, principals can build awareness with the following questions.

- What are the Mathematical Practices?
- Why are they important for our students?
- How do we use the Mathematical Practices in our instruction?

Understanding the structure and vocabulary of the mathematics standards is an important step for leaders and teachers as they work together to implement the CCSS. Figure 1.3 defines the key terms used in the CCSS and identifies the standards for one of the domains in grades 3–5.

Rigor in the Standards

Knowing how rigor is built into the CCSS will enable collaborative teams to see how the developers of the standards respond to the readiness challenges that U.S. students are facing in their college and career lives. In both ELA/literacy and mathematics, the standards provide a unique, new approach to the role of rigor in the classroom. With their emphasis on students' thinking skills, the new standards eschew the idea that rigor comes from increased amounts of work, including assignments of a larger number of homework problems, longer reading hours, and more take-home essays. Instead, the emphasis is placed on developing the quality of student thinking applied within daily work.

Rigor in English Language Arts

For teachers implementing the ELA/literacy standards, it is helpful to start the discussion of rigor with an inquiry about text complexity. Anchor standard ten (CCRA.R.10) in the domain Range of Reading and Text Complexity in the Reading strand states, "Read and comprehend complex literary and informational texts independently and proficiently" (NGA & CCSSO, 2010b, p. 10). The CCSS define *text complexity* as "the inherent difficulty of reading and comprehending a text combined with a consideration of the reader and the task variables" (NGA & CCSSO, 2010c, p. 43). This emphasis on text complexity has created a lot of discussion within the English language arts community.

If teachers come to collaborative team meetings having reviewed their grade-level standards, their first investigation can be an examination of text complexity using questions such as the following.

- What is text complexity?
- Why is it important?
- How can we make sure to select age-appropriate text?
- How can we raise the level of students' ability to deal with complex text?
- How are the ELA standards laid out so that text complexity intensifies from year to year?

Standards define what students should understand and be able to do.

Clusters summarize groups of related standards. Note that standards from different clusters may sometimes be closely related because mathematics is a connected subject.

Domains are larger groups of related standards. Standards from different domains may sometimes be closely related. The domains apply to mathematics content in grades K–8. The domains for grades 3–5 are Operations and Algebraic Thinking, Number and Operations in Base Ten, Number and Operations—Fractions, Measurement and Data, and Geometry.

Conceptual categories are the areas for high school (grades 9–12) mathematics content standards. The six conceptual categories are: Number and Quantity (N), Algebra (A), Functions (F), Modeling, Geometry (G), and Statistics and Probability (S). Each conceptual category with the exception of Modeling has domains and clusters. For example, Number and Quantity has five domains: The Real Number System (N–RN), Quantities (N–Q), The Complete Number System (N–CN), and Vector and Matrix Quantities (N–VM). The domain The Real Number System has two clusters: Extend the properties of exponents to rational components and Use properties of rational and irrational numbers.

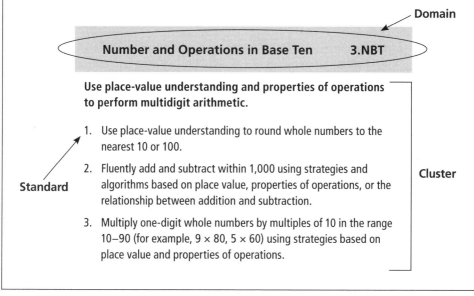

Figure 1.3: How to read the grade-level mathematics standards.

Source: Adapted from NGA & CCSSO, 2010e, pp. 5, 57, 59, and 60.

*Visit **go.solution-tree.com/leadership** for a reproducible version of this figure.*

Understanding text complexity is important for all teachers, not just those with advanced reading coursework in English or reading. It is essential that teachers in non-ELA disciplines also develop and use this know-how. Defining text complexity with appropriate grade-level examples from literature and informational text is essential to selecting the most appropriate reading materials in each classroom. Appendix B of the Common Core ELA/literacy is a useful resource for all teachers: it provides examples of texts for all grade bands—K–1, 2–3, 4–5, 6–8, 9–10, and 11–CCR (NGA & CCSSO, 2010d). Qualitative evaluation of text allows teachers to place texts on a spectrum. This spectrum allows teachers to set up a developmental pattern that places increasingly more difficult texts in front of students as the year progresses. This action aligns with the concept that each standard is designed for end-of-year proficiency with students proceeding from easy text to more difficult text as they practice and acquire new skills.

For example, such middle-grade texts as *Little Women* and *The Adventures of Tom Sawyer* can be placed in a 1–2 rank order of complexity. An analysis of *The Adventures of Tom Sawyer* will show it is the more complex text because it is written in 1840s Missourian dialect. By adopting this rank order strategy with other texts within a year's reading assignment, teachers can plan instruction intentionally using texts that move from simple to complex as they develop students' skills over time. To assess text complexity, teachers include qualitative evaluations by assessing a book's levels of meaning, vocabulary, word relationships and patterns, sentence and paragraph structures, syntax, conventions, author style, genre, and even the author's logic (NGA & CCSSO, 2010c). These aspects of text complexity are often developed in the standards in the Language strand (NGA & CCSSO, 2010b). In more complex reading materials, these elements challenge the students. Teachers can also use readability measures to supplement the qualitative dimensions with quantitative information. This information combined with considerations about the reader and the task enables teachers to support students climbing the challenge staircase. As the students climb that staircase, they extend the reach of their ever-developing cognitive skills. Principals can guide their teachers' adoption of this using the reproducible "Assessing Text Complexity" (page 41) to evaluate a text's complexity.

Text complexity is only one factor in the 21st century definition of rigor. Noting that text complexity, not text length, is the key determinant of intellectual rigor, principals can lead grade-level teams to see where the standards themselves are positioned on the staircase. In this way, teachers can see how rigor is added to the standards as each one becomes more demanding with each grade level. In addition, teachers can look at standards in the other strands to find the parallel connections that will allow them to layer skills from several strands in a single lesson or project.

Table 1.2 shows how point of view develops across grades 3 through 6 in the Reading Standards for Literature. Notice the increased rigor of the standard as students move through the grades. For example, in third grade, the standard centers on the ability of the students to identify their own point of view and distinguish it from that of the narrator. By sixth grade, the standard expects students to know what "point of view" means and be able to explain how an author develops it in a text.

Table 1.2: Literature Standards for Domain Craft and Structure, Grades 3–6

CCR Anchor Standard	Grade 3 Standard	Grade 4 Standard	Grade 5 Standard	Grade 6 Standard
CCRA.R.6: *Assess* how point of view or purpose shapes the content and style of a text.	**RL.3.6:** *Distinguish* their own point of view from that of the narrator or those of the characters.	**RL.4.6:** *Compare and contrast* the point of view from which different stories are narrated, including the difference between first- and third-person narrations.	**RL.5.6:** *Describe* how a narrator's or speaker's point of view influences how events are described.	**RL.6.6:** *Explain* how an author develops the point of view of the narrator or speaker in a text.

Source: Adapted from NGA & CCSSO, 2010b, pp. 12 and 36.

This table illustrates the last and perhaps most important factor about rigor in the CCSS ELA/literacy. The verbs—*assess, distinguish, compare and contrast, describe,* and *explain*—are representative of actions throughout the standards. Unlike the verbs *recall* or *understand*, which allow students to depend on memorized responses for what they *know*, these verbs challenge students to show what they can *do* with text as they demonstrate their proficiencies as higher-level thinkers.

Rigor in Mathematics

Although the Common Core mathematics standards are fewer and more concentrated, they are no less rigorous. The introduction to these standards accentuates the importance of grasping the purpose of the new mathematics standards and the intentional shift in mathematics practice (NGA & CCSSO, 2010e). In line with the *PISA 2012 Mathematics Framework* (OECD, 2010a), these standards are attempting to improve U.S. students' performance in an area of international testing that shows U.S. students to be less-than-average performers. The Mathematical Practices highlight the importance of problem solving, not as the *end product* in mathematics or as *procedures* for students to memorize, but as the core *process* for thinking mathematically about rich and deep mathematics. Furthermore, the introduction highlights that problem solving is not a sequential list of steps to be memorized and checked off one step at a time, but a collection of critical- and creative-thinking skills that are intertwined and developed as proficiencies to be used in the problem-solving process (NGA & CCSSO, 2010e). During a classroom walkthrough, a principal should note how teachers connect the day's lesson with one or more of the Mathematical Practices. Similarly, a principal should note the teacher's use of instructional strategies that advance students' understanding of those practices.

From the perspective of rigor, the mathematics standards are like the ELA/literacy standards in that both begin most often with a simple verb that drives the thinking processes. *Prove* is the numerical champion in the mathematics standards. In addition, that verb calls on students to complete more and more complex mathematical tasks and then to show how and why they made their proofs in a certain way. From the earliest grades, the leading mathematics verb in each standard calls on students to develop understanding of concepts as they proceed from the concrete world of number operations to the abstractions of probability. Just as in the ELA standards, these verbs are the engines that push and pull student cognition into the more and more complex thinking required. As students learn how to *estimate, represent, interpret, distinguish, reason, construct,* and *critique* and become increasingly proficient in the most common thinking skills included in the standards, they are better able to delve into deeper learning of the content (Pellegrino & Hilton, 2012). By attending to the importance of these key higher-order thinking verbs, teachers will find they must pay explicit attention to the development of students' mathematical thinking and problem-solving proficiencies. Gone are the days when students with strong memories could rise to the top without understanding the mathematical concepts delineated in the curriculum. In regard to the Common Core standards, it becomes essential that principals provide teachers with the preparation, support, and feedback that enable all teachers to be intentional about advancing the higher-order thinking skills called for in the mathematics as well as the English language arts standards.

Why Are the CCSS Important?

Answers to this question help teachers unpack their understanding of the standards as well as explain the shift from the individual state standards to the CCSS. Most important, teachers will see how the question's answers set the stage for responses to the third question, How will our school embrace the CCSS?

NGA and CCSSO make clear that the CCSS are meant to replace the outdated standards from the individual states. The authors' aim is to empower U.S. schools to prepare all students equitably for college and career in the 21st century global economy without differences in expectations across states. This means that 21st century students will be better prepared to compete with students from other states and nations for seats in higher-education classrooms and the ever-changing job market (Bellanca & Brandt, 2010; Bellanca, Fogarty, & Pete, 2012). International tests as well as a plethora of well-articulated academic, business, and governmental organizations' studies indicate that U.S. students already trail behind in several competitive domains; reports from other nations such as Australia, Brazil, and Finland indicate that they do not intend to stand pat, but are already improving their own education systems (Atkin et al., 2010; Barber & Mourshed, 2007).

What will well-prepared, job-competitive 21st century students look and sound like? What will be their most notable characteristics? The Standards for Mathematical Practice identify the eight characteristics that fit the bill (see pages 20–24). As a result of their studies, the 21st century mathematics–ready students will be capable problem solvers equipped with habits of mind that include the abilities to reason abstractly, apply mathematical understandings to new situations, use precise language, and construct viable arguments, as well as persevere in a variety of other mathematical activities.

In English language arts and other disciplines that use the ELA/literacy standards, students who meet the standards will show a mastery of close-reading strategies and be critical readers, writers, and speakers in an age of information. They will do so with "cogent reasoning and use of evidence that is essential to both private deliberation and responsible citizenship in a democratic republic" (NGA & CCSSO, 2010b, p. 3). Comparisons with other nations' school systems' emphasis on students learning to read informational text show that U.S. students are coming up short in quantity and quality (see Mullis, Martin, Foy, & Drucker, 2012). Given the increased emphasis on ability to read informational text, especially in college, the amount of such text use and the ability of teachers from different disciplines to guide students' study with informational text, both print and digital, cannot be ignored.

How Will Our School Embrace the CCSS?

Change is all over the place. Principals and their leadership teams have to deal daily with downpours of change. Students come and go. Students grow up. Students transfer. Teachers retire, and new blood arrives almost as quickly as the seasons. New research appears. Old fads die. Life is change. School life is perpetual change.

How a principal manages school change will say a great deal about the future of the students in that school. When the change portends to cause a major shift, such as the arrival of the Common Core State Standards, the key to success is found in principals' use of innovative thinking to solve the big and little problems these new directives add to their full plates and the delegation of responsibility for ensuring that all elements of the change occur. They have many leadership choices to make.

When faced with implementing the CCSS, principals use the first *how* to focus on the overall method they will adopt to bring the Common Core into their schools. A transition is to be made—a move from the old way of doing business to a new way. In spite of those false prophets who claim the new standards are no different, the CCSS *are* different. They signal the growing changes in how U.S. schools must prepare students for a new century. The one-room schoolhouse is obsolete. So too are the factory-model schools of the 20th century with their heavy, one-sided emphasis on basic skills.

How principals elect to make the move will mean a great deal. The changes will not be easy, but there are options on the transition-to-transformation spectrum. At one end of the spectrum sits the Replication and Duplication (R&D) method. At the other sits the Renovation and Innovation (R&I) approach. Additional choices are in between. The innovative problem solvers will not settle for a one-size-fits-all package deal. Those principals will examine the options and personalize the change process to fit the needs of their individual schools while keeping an eye on the future demands for students' competencies. In the midst of this, principals who can delegate to a leadership team with differentiated assignments are more likely to succeed.

Replication and Duplication (R&D)

The R&D method calls for *replication and duplication* of what has worked in the past. Its goal is nondisruptive transition. It is the easiest change model but fails to meet the real purposes of the Common Core. Leonardo da Vinci certainly would have laughed at such work. If the principal merely finds and copies a plan from a school that uses the standards well and asks teachers to review their current practices and answer the question, "What is it that we are already doing with our current objectives over which we can cut and paste the CCSS?" it allows the team to say, "We have done the job. We have alignment." Over several weeks, every teacher proceeds to cut and paste until his or her lessons are properly headed with one or more Common Core standard. They then return to their classrooms, shut the door, and continue teaching much as always with no changes that reflect the CCSS.

Renovation and Innovation (R&I)

In contrast, the R&I method calls for *renovation and innovation*. Its goal is transformation. Its means are the mindful, productive strategies of creative thinking à la Leonardo da Vinci, that dare the educational leader to look ahead for a novel set of answers. The purpose of this new set is to empower teachers to make significant and substantive changes in what and how they teach aided by their deep grasp of the CCSS.

Because transformational R&I asks the principals, leaders, and teachers to make personal paradigm shifts in how they view teaching and learning, R&I can be the toughest change model to implement. It invites teachers to look at a new standard and ask many, many questions, such as the following.

- "How much of what I do will allow me to realign my practice with the balanced instruction the CCSS suggest?"

- "How far out of my comfort zone am I willing to go?"

- "How do I provide explicit instruction for the thinking skills that are dominant at that grade?"

- "What does it mean to *analyze*?"

- "What does it mean to *compare*?"

- "What makes a strong synthesis?"

- "How do I prepare students to carry out tasks with which they are not familiar?"

- "What strategies do I use to help students use these skills and strategies with the tougher texts they are reading or the harder mathematics problems they are solving?"

FIFTH-GRADE WRITING STANDARD IN DOMAIN TEXT TYPES AND PURPOSES

CCRA.W.3: Write narratives to develop real or imagined experiences or events using effective technique, well-chosen details, and well-structured event sequences.

W.5.3: Write narratives to develop real or imagined experiences or events using effective technique, descriptive details, and clear event sequences.

  a. Orient the reader by establishing a situation and introducing a narrator and characters; organize an event sequence that unfolds naturally.

  b. Use narrative techniques, such as dialogue, description, and pacing, to develop experiences and events or show the responses of the characters to situations.

  c. Use a variety of transitional words, phrases, and clauses to manage the sequence of events.

  d. Use concrete words and phrases and sensory details to convey experiences and events precisely.

  e. Provide a conclusion that follows from the narrated experiences or events.

Source: Adapted from NGA & CCSSO, 2010b, pp. 18 and 20.

When renovating and innovating, individual teachers have to assess their practice to determine how it fits with the Common Core and to seek out new aligned instructional strategies. In ELA, renovation calls for teachers to align all parts of each grade-level standard into the curriculum. Consider the implications of implementing a standard at the fifth-grade level from the domain Text Types and Purposes in the Writing strand. The standard consists of five parts (a–e), each of which teachers should consider when developing lessons to teach students how to write narratives.

The multitude of questions teachers will encounter may make many of them uncomfortable. Some will flee. Others will fight. However, the same can be said of their students as the instructional paradigm of them being passive recipients switches to them generating ideas. You are the controller of information. You are the problem solver. You are the worker. To work effectively with teachers and students as they cope with the paradigm shift, leaders must be innovative and resilient.

Innovation calls for the most comprehensive of shifts. To succeed in this transformation, school leaders often arrange for teachers to work together in a whole-school approach intended to make significant and substantive changes in teaching and learning. Teachers collaborate in grade-level or subject teams to unpack the relevant standards with a focus on the outcomes or results of instruction. They strive to set aside conventional practices such as covering content in a mathematics textbook, relying on familiar and favorite stories or novels, or grading a set number of writing assignments. Managing this shift means there is little room for one step at a time. Random acts of individual change in the number of facts students are able to recall don't qualify. The desired outcomes include (1) use of complex thinking and problem-solving skills that match with the selected standards, (2) understanding of the content element of each standard targeted, and (3) evidence of how well students' performance aligns with the standards.

Those principals who want the teachers to move out of ineffective and obsolete teaching methods and make these changes play an important role in facilitating teachers' paradigm shifts that reveal their own deeper thinking. It is not enough for principals to stand on the side and let teachers sink or swim. Here the principals bring the essence of da Vinci into play by acting on those leadership qualities that were introduced at the start of this chapter (see page 15). When this occurs, the principals' supervisors will see observables that signal, "This is leadership for change. This is how innovation happens. This is walking the talk. This is innovative leadership."

How does innovative leadership look and sound as principals spark creative thinking, problem solving, deeper understanding of content, and improved assessment? Consider these examples.

- "That's a great idea. I understand you may feel uncomfortable doing math this way. We need to try it. I am not going to give you a bad evaluation if it doesn't work on the spot."

- "I know making these switches to informational text will take work. That is why I am saying it's OK for you to leave out those other books and give more time to the Informational Text standards."

- "I'm giving your team the authority to decide how you will restructure mathematics time. And I want you to test out your ideas and make sure they do work."

- "I am really pleased to see how well you are working together to include explicit instruction for critical thinking about the social studies material in the standards. I know that is a challenge."

- "I can't help but notice the risks you are taking to add these digital tools. I see you making great combinations of the standards for writing with the call for digital media."

- "I stand with you. I want to see you taking the risk to try this new approach with the Reading standards. And I also want to see you try more of your formative assessments so you have data for your decisions."

- "Invite me into your classroom. I would love to see the kids' presentations and how you've aligned them with standards in the Speaking and Listening strand."

- "I agree with you. From my understanding of the mathematics standards, it is not just memorizing a procedure. It's about practice. And practice is about the transfer that shows deeper learning of the content."

- "I would only add two suggestions to my list of pluses. First, I would like to see students doing more self-assessments before you give them feedback especially on the thinking they did to prove those equations. Second, I would like to see a tighter alignment of the final written summary to the standard."

- "I like the way this team thinks outside the box. Your science, technology, engineering, and mathematics [STEM] project-based learning [PBL] plan is unusual but I think you've aligned it well with both the STEM elements and the ELA Speaking and Listening strand. I can't wait to see how it goes."

Elementary teams adopting the R&I approach may start with the ELA performance tasks described in appendix B of the Common Core (NGA & CCSSO, 2010c). These tasks, based on the Reading standards, provide examples for teachers to identify how students demonstrate how well they can do the thinking that is called for in a standard. Figure 1.4 (page 34) presents selected sample performance tasks for informational texts.

Sample performance task: Students determine the meaning of domain-specific words or phrases, such as crust, mantle, magma, and lava, and important general-academic words and phrases that appear in Seymour Simon's *Volcanoes*.

RI.4.4: Determine the meaning of general-academic and domain-specific words or phrases in a text relevant to a grade 4 topic or subject area.

Sample performance task: Students determine the main idea of Colin A. Ronan's "Telescopes" and create a *summary by explaining how key details support* his distinctions regarding different types of telescopes.

RI.4.2: Determine the main idea of a text and explain how it is supported by key details; summarize the text.

Figure 1.4: Sample performance tasks for informational text in grade 4.
Source: Adapted from NGA & CCSSO, 2010b, p. 14; NGA & CCSSO, 2010c, p. 76.

By identifying how the students' performance looks or sounds at the close of the school year, the teacher teams can create full-year curriculum maps, continually moving backward in each unit plan. In each unit plan, they also start at the end with the performance assessments and work their way all the way backward through each daily lesson plan. As a result, they can start the year with less complex literature and informational text and advance to the more challenging text at year's end. To assist with this flow, teachers can preview the given sample performance tasks in appendix B of the Common Core ELA and create their own performance tasks aligning each piece of literature or text with the final, desired competencies.

By creating a single rubric first to make formative assessments of students' progress and ultimately the final summative assessment, the teams can build a consistent database that shows how their students develop the skills through the year. A simple, student-friendly, well-constructed formative rubric given prior to the first reading assignment will help all students know the full expectations and have the chance to self-assess their progress from the start of the school year to the end. At various check points through the school year, the teacher can rely on the same rubric, even as the complexity of the texts and reading challenge increase, to measure each student's progress and give the appropriate constructive feedback that will enable improvement. By the third quarter's end with use of this single, guiding rubric to track development, teachers should have an accurate picture of who needs a final super push to reach the standard and who is able to fly above and beyond the mark.

For example, a formative rubric based on the seventh-grade reading literature standard, "Analyze how particular elements of a story or drama interact (for example, how setting shapes the characters or plot)" (RL.7.3; NGA & CCSSO, 2010b, p. 36), guides students in understanding the thinking approach they take as they analyze the text. If these students know how to examine each part and identify the connections that exist, they will do well. They will do better if they understand all the possible connections—literal and figurative. If their analytic skill is weak, they will need guidance.

To construct a student-friendly guiding rubric, teachers select the standard on which they want to focus for the school year. They build the standard's benchmarks by delineating their expectations of what students must be able to do at year's end. These then become a tool that starts with students' self-assessment of those behaviors. In the case of this example, the guiding rubric "Analysis of Connections in Literature" focuses on each of the parts of a story that interact or connect—characters, plot, theme, and so on (see **go.solution.tree.com/leadership** for an online-only reproducible of this rubric).

After teachers have clarified the performance outcomes, they are ready to select the strategies that will be most powerful as the driving forces to increasing achievement and deeper learning. It is best if teachers initially select evidence-based strategies that will have the best chance for developing those critical- and creative-thinking skills positioned in each standard statement.

Some strategies like project-based learning, problem-based learning, and explicit instruction of thinking skills hold the strongest promise for moving students to the deeper learning that drives the highest achievement (Pellegrino & Hilton, 2012) and work best within the CCSS framework but are not the easiest to implement. These strategies, which teachers strengthen using inquiry, graphic organizers, and hypothetical thinking, are not quick fixes. If teachers are most comfortable with handing out worksheets, lecturing, or using direct instruction, they will find that such outdated, ineffective, and shallow learning strategies are the ones most poorly aligned with achieving the CCSS expectations for deeper thinking and problem solving. Thus, when it comes time to measure progress with their new performance assessments, teachers who accept the challenges to adopt more complex instructional models will see the most dramatic gains among their students who perform what they know.

Once again, it is important to note the principal's role in helping teachers adopt or expand the strategies that are most effective. In addition to creating a culture in the school in which teachers feel safe to make the called-for shifts in how they think and teach, the principal who wants to see innovation in action will continue interacting with supportive and encouraging words and actions. In addition, this principal will make careful, focused professional development choices that form professional learning communities with a multiyear focus on mastering the strategies that will most help teachers implement their innovative standards-aligned instruction, curriculum, and assessment. In this role, the principal will spend a majority of his or her time and effort mentoring, coaching, and assessing the quality of standards-driven innovation that occurs in each classroom.

A New Paradigm

What strategies best align with the CCSS and are most likely to produce the greatest gains in student performance? The first indicator of effective strategies comes from the United States' major global competitor, Australia. Australia has consistently scored among the top three nations on the Programme for International Student Assessment (OECD, 2009).

How does Australia do this? A clue is found in how its educational leaders give top priority to the development of quality teaching that results in deeper learning. While Australia understands accountability, its teacher assessment practices don't hold teachers and students hostage with an overemphasis on tests, measurements, and punitive legislation—actions geared to propping in place outdated approaches to teaching and learning. Instead, Australia, like Finland and the other top-performing nations, stresses developing teachers' readiness with a curriculum heavy on 21st century skills.

The Government of South Australia has assumed an international leadership position in stressing the importance of teaching for effective learning. Its latest work points out the value it places on maintaining its forefront position in the global education community. Seeking guidance from such U.S. experts as Jay McTighe, Grant Wiggins, Geoffrey and Renate Caine, Susan Chambers-Otero, Robin Fogarty, Brian Pete, and George Otero, South Australia's Department of Education and Children's Services spent five years creating a groundbreaking framework for effective teaching. This framework aligns with the others that Australian states like Queensland and New South Wales have developed. The South Australia Department of Education and Children's Services created two guides—the framework guide and a resources handbook—for every teacher and principal (Atkin, 2011; Atkin et al., 2010). These resources reflect the message, "Minds are not mechanisms: they are organisms. And organisms are not assembled; they grow" (Atkin et al., 2010, p. 9).

The second indicator of practices that best align with the CCSS ELA/literacy and mathematics comes from six areas of best practice research, mostly gathered in the United States. A review of these practices reveals that these same practices also show up in the Australian report.

1. High-effects strategies designed within explicit instruction models (Marzano, 2009a)

2. Close reading of complex text (Piercy, 2011)

3. Concept-rich mathematics instruction (Ben-Hur, 2006)

4. Inquiry-rich project-based learning (Ravitz, 2009) and problem-based learning (OECD, 2010b)

5. Integrated technology tools (Metiri Group, 2008)

6. Deeper learning for transfer (Pellegrino & Hilton, 2012)

These strategies have well-documented research bases. Each fits within the five criteria outlined in the CCSS. The Common Core State Standards define the rigorous skills and knowledge in English language arts and mathematics that need to be effectively taught and learned for students to be ready to succeed academically in credit-bearing, college-entry courses and in workforce training programs. These standards drive effective policy and practice, align with college and work expectations, include rigorous content and application of knowledge through higher-order skills, meet international benchmarks, and demonstrate research- and evidence-based practices.

Each standard necessitates that teachers spend time not only learning about the strategies of choice but also planning when to integrate the strategies into lessons, units, and projects aligned with the standards and receive coached practice time and peer support for implementation. After all, as da Vinci demonstrated, innovation takes the time, the reflection, and the willingness to find a better way.

Looking Back

Leonardo da Vinci's last known home and workshop at Château du Clos Lucé sits in the middle of a great green park near the Loire (Khan, 2009). Copies of his large inventions dot the landscape. The smaller models are housed in the castle along with many sketches and work artifacts. This was a man who could not sit still. His prodigious mind was facilitated by his endless quest to find answers to a multitude of unanswered questions. This was a mind that never just accumulated or stored knowledge: it was a mind that created new knowledge from connections that never before had been made. No problem was too great for him to solve and no field of study too difficult. His very disposition was to make answers. Thus, he stands as the archetypical standard for all whose work is centered on solving an endless parade of problems. Twenty-first century principals face an endless parade of problems. They are now asked to take on a new problem—implementation of the Common Core State Standards—and guide their school teams to new solutions that first, last, and always benefit their students, each and every one.

Discussion Questions

The discussion questions are for collaborative, grade-level, or department teams or even just two colleagues working together or with a principal as part of a staff meeting to discuss this chapter as part of a book study or as a stand-alone chapter with good information and examples for rigorous and relevant learning. There is nothing as powerful as reflective conversation among professionals.

1. How will you respond to the question, What are the Common Core State Standards?

2. Give an example of text complexity that includes some of the elements described in the reproducible "Assessing Text Complexity" (page 41).

3. Do you agree with the assertions made in the discussion of the question, Why are the CCSS important? Why? Why not?

4. In what ways do the R&I and R&D methods differ? How is R&I transforming while R&D is more about transitioning? Which approach characterizes change actions in your school?

5. How familiar with the CCSS are teachers in your school? Which teachers —English language arts / literacy or mathematics—do you think will most readily embrace the CCSS? Do you think the teachers' grade-level assignments will be a factor in their willingness to embrace the CCSS?

Takeaways

In a final look back, consider the following takeaways for this chapter. These are just some of the learnings that will benefit you as you support, observe, and evaluate great instruction.

What are the Common Core State Standards?

- Self-assessment for innovative leadership qualities

- Organization of new national standards across forty-five states

Why are the CCSS important?

- Raise the rigor and relevance for preparing students for college and career

- Develop self-reliance

How will our school embrace the CCSS?

- Transition through Replication and Duplication (R&D)

    OR

- Transformation through Renovation and Innovation (R&I)

- Teaching for deeper learning

A Common Core Planning Framework

What is our school's driving or focus question?

What do we know about the Common Core State Standards?

Why are the CCSS important?

How can we best transition to implementing the standards?

What steps will we take toward transformation?

Standards for Mathematical Practice

Mathematical Practice 1

Make sense of problems and persevere in solving them.

Mathematical Practice 2

Reason abstractly and quantitatively.

Mathematical Practice 3

Construct viable arguments and critique the reasoning of others.

Mathematical Practice 4

Model with mathematics.

Mathematical Practice 5

Use appropriate tools strategically.

Mathematical Practice 6

Attend to precision.

Mathematical Practice 7

Look for and make use of structure.

Mathematical Practice 8

Look for and express regularity in repeated reasoning.

Source: NGA & CCSSO, 2010e, pp. 6–8.

Assessing Text Complexity

Assessing text complexity is an important task for leaders and teachers as they select more challenging reading materials for the students. This tool provides a framework for examining resources for reading instruction.

☐ **Grade** ☐ **Students** ☐ **All** ☐ **Group** ☐ **Individual**

Reading Standard for Literature: _____

Reading Standard for Informational Text: _____

Author: _____ **Text:** _____ **Genre:** _____

Books previously read in class or assigned to students: _____

_____

Teacher: _____ Date: _____

Readability Measure

Name: _____ Score: _____

Quantitative readability measures describe aspects of text complexity such as word length and frequency, sentence length, and text cohesion. Some familiar readability measures include the Lexile Framework for Reading, the Dale-Chall Readability Formula, and the Flesch-Kincaid Grade Level Test.

Reading Complexity

Check all that apply relevant to grade-level average.

Level of Meaning

☐ Low ☐ At grade level ☐ High ☐ Challenging

Vocabulary

☐ Low ☐ At grade level ☐ High ☐ Challenging

Word Relationships and Patterns

☐ Low ☐ At grade level ☐ High ☐ Challenging

Sentence and Paragraph Structure

☐ Low ☐ At grade level ☐ High ☐ Challenging

page 1 of 2

Syntax

☐ Low   ☐ At grade level   ☐ High   ☐ Challenging

Conventions

☐ Low   ☐ At grade level   ☐ High   ☐ Challenging

Author's Style

☐ Low   ☐ At grade level   ☐ High   ☐ Challenging

Author's Logic

☐ Low   ☐ At grade level   ☐ High   ☐ Challenging

Comments:

_____
_____
_____
_____
_____
_____
_____
_____
_____
_____
_____
_____
_____
_____
_____
_____
_____
_____
_____
_____
_____
_____

School Leader's Guide to the Common Core © 2013 Solution Tree Press • solution-tree.com
Visit **go.solution-tree.com/leadership** to download this page.

CHAPTER 2

The Shift in Implementation

Sustaining Professional Learning

Leadership and learning are indispensable to each other.

—John F. Kennedy

There is an expression in the men's clothing business: "The most expensive suit a man can buy is the suit that he only wears once." Extrapolating from that idea, you can say, "The most expensive staff development is that which teachers do not transfer to their classrooms." With that metaphor in mind, school leaders working with the Common Core are mindful of the value of sound professional learning opportunities that have long-lasting impact on instruction. They can shape those professional experiences with elements and conditions that maximize transfer from the classroom.

The success of professional learning can only be determined by measuring the implementation of strategies, incorporation of concepts, and changes in attitudes that teachers are able to transfer from the staffroom to the classroom.

Too many times, professional learning is judged based on evaluations teachers fill out at the end of a session as they are packing up their bags and collecting their car keys. As leaders and teachers shift their thinking about the goals of professional learning, they understand that success is measured by the number and level of applications in the classroom that result from the professional development sessions.

The rule about peer coaching or collegial conversations mirrors what is expected from teachers when teaching the CCSS. No longer can teachers concern themselves just with covering their content and prepping for the test. They have to take time to go deeper and delve more rigorously into rich, complex content. The same is true for principals and other school leaders implementing the Common Core. The success of professional learning is no longer measured by how many teachers attend prerequisite sessions over a period of time but by tangible proof that teachers are applying new ideas, concepts, or strategies that they learn in well-designed professional development activities.

The role of the instructional leader is to promote the learning and success of *all* students through the teachers' instructional excellence. A more dynamic way to describe the shift is to say, "The leaders promote learning for a lifetime, not for the test." In the era of the Common Core State Standards, this description emphasizes the shift to promoting the rigorous application of relevant learning processes that prepare students for success in college or career. To achieve these high-stakes results, school leaders must lead the way through sustained and job-embedded professional support for teachers.

In this chapter, we describe three ways in which principals and other school leaders can work collaboratively with teachers to implement the CCSS: (1) leading by example, (2) providing sound professional development, and (3) embracing professional learning communities.

Leading by Example

The Common Core State Standards require a more rigorous approach to the teaching and learning equation to ensure that the expectations for student achievement are accomplished and demonstrated in assessments. It is not enough to prepare students to choose the best possible answer from a multiple-choice test or to closely follow the formula for writing a paragraph that fits a prescribed rubric. The CCSS emphasize the processes of learning such as higher-order thinking skills and authentic application. The sample performance tasks in appendix B of the CCSS (NGA & CCSSO, 2010c) provide numerous examples of this focus. The shift in emphasis on learning processes is evident in a comparison of the language in a 2004 New Jersey state standard and a comparable Common Core standard. (See figure 2.1.)

The traditional standard requires the student to produce oral and written work to demonstrate understanding of informational text; however, it does not specify the form for which the student provides evidence of understanding. The Common Core standard expresses the expectation explicitly: the student must *find and identify* two or more central ideas, *analyze* their development throughout the text, and *summarize* the text, or more specifically, *objectively summarize* the text. This expectation is a dramatic shift from the language of state standards familiar to many teachers through standardized testing.

New Jersey State Standard 3.1.7 H: Inquiry and Research

1. Produce written work and oral work that demonstrate comprehension of informational materials.

CCSS Informational Text Standard for Domain Key Ideas and Details, Grade 7

RI.7.2: Determine two or more central ideas in a text and analyze their development over the course of the text; provide an objective summary of the text.

Figure 2.1: Comparison of a state standard and a Common Core standard.
Source: New Jersey Department of Education, 2004, p. C–18; NGA & CCSSO, 2010b, p. 39.

To help their staff understand the gravity of this shift, effective leaders take every opportunity to do more than "talk the talk." They "walk the walk" by being able to demonstrate the differences in expectations between the familiar state standards and the Common Core State Standards. Collaborative meetings provide the settings for leaders to capitalize on those *teachable moments* to communicate through modeling what is expected in the classroom. In essence, the principal or school leader has a chance to *model* the model of active, engaged learning strategies. The responsibility for creating understanding of the CCSS can be shared among members of the leadership team. For instance, at each collaborative team meeting, someone from the leadership team presents information about the Common Core. This content becomes the standards-based curriculum that teachers develop as they implement the Common Core ELA/literacy and mathematics standards. Much like modeling scenarios with students in the classroom, leaders must share this information with the teachers in ways that enhance understanding and foster acceptance of change. How leaders present the information determines how well the teachers gain knowledge and experience and how able they are to apply their learning in their practice.

School leaders' time is fractured. They interact with students, staff, parents, district administrators, and community members. Consequently, leaders need to plan carefully to make the best use of the time in faculty meetings. These meetings can matter more when used as opportunities for leaders to demonstrate interactive teaching models in an effort to counteract the stand-and-deliver tradition that is overused in classrooms as well as professional development sessions. Ironically, the widely accepted practice of engaging teaching models for students is not always apparent in professional development activities for teachers. Knowing this, effective principals and other instructional leaders value the meeting time with staff as teachable moments to model the look-fors they want to see when they are visiting classrooms.

Modeling Desired Look-Fors

Here is one simple example of how a principal could model a required CCSS thinking strategy that could then be transferred from the staffroom to the classroom. The content is from the Standards for Mathematical Practice, which describe varieties of expertise that mathematics educators at all levels seek to develop in their students. The principal wants the staff to be familiar with these practices as they spiral through grades K–12 in the CCSS for mathematics. Just like a classroom teacher who has to teach some content, the principal is faced with the decision of how to cover the content.

Normally, a principal would read the list of eight Mathematical Practices or pass out the list and maybe have the teachers read along as he or she comments on each practice (see page 40 for the reproducible "Standards for Mathematical Practice," or visit **go.solution-tree.com/leadership**). A more effective approach is one that engages the teachers in discussions leading them to make decisions about the importance of the practices in their mathematics instruction. In this approach, the leader shows the list of practices on a whiteboard and asks the teachers to work in pairs or small groups to discuss which practice is most important for students at their grade level. In this collaborative task, the teachers have to read all eight Mathematical Practices, evaluate them in the context of instruction at the grade level they teach, and justify their choice. To summarize the results of the groups' discussions, the leader does a rank and tally of the eight practices by a show of hands. This activity reveals the extent of agreement about which practices are considered most important and provides opportunity for further discussion about what will be needed to implement the practices.

In this example, the teachers, as learners, engage in the thinking skill of *evaluation*, the highest level in Bloom's Taxonomy. They also *collaborate* with each other and *communicate* their ideas. Collaboration and communication skills are included in the college and career readiness anchor standards for the Speaking and Listening strand of the Common Core ELA/literacy.

Comparing and Contrasting Instruction

The principal or leader extends the discussion by *comparing* and *contrasting* how he or she taught the content using a cooperative learning structure and higher-order thinking rather than a traditional direct instruction model.

At this point, the meeting could be considered a success, but the goal of the principal, and all teachers, is to teach to the point of application. After observing and commenting on the ranking of practices according to importance, the leader asks the teachers to work again with their partners to discuss how they would use the same approach with their students. This two- or three-minute conversation specifically about *transfer* from the staffroom to the classroom is a vital part of professional development that is many times overlooked. The group comes together again to share ideas about using the approach with students. This structure for a professional development activity reinforces the idea that the principal is an instructional leader who models the look-fors he or she wants to see teachers using in their classrooms.

SELECTED CCRAS FOR SPEAKING AND LISTENING STRAND

Domain: Comprehension and Collaboration

CCRA.SL.1: Prepare for and participate effectively in a range of conversations and collaborations with diverse partners, building on others' ideas and expressing their own clearly and persuasively.

Domain: Presentation of Knowledge and Ideas

CCRA.SL.4: Present information, findings, and supporting evidence such that listeners can follow the line of reasoning and the organization, development, and style are appropriate to task, purpose, and audience.

Source: NGA & CCSSO, 2010b, p. 22.

Because time and resources are becoming increasingly scarce, it is important that school leaders take advantage of key opportunities with teachers to support them with sound instructional strategies that they in turn can use to engage students in different ways.

Providing Sound Professional Development

For schools to implement the Common Core, the principal has to become a connoisseur of professional development, and a true connoisseur knows how to recognize effective staff development by looking for the following three elements.

1. Best practices in professional learning (Fogarty & Pete, 2007)

2. Elements of design for adult learners (Knowles, 1973)

3. Peer coaching to support professional learning (Joyce & Showers, 2002)

Joellen Killion (2012) notes, "Successful principals shape the culture of schools, set clear expectations, and share leadership with others to create productive learning environments for students and staff" (p. 4).

Best Practices in Professional Development

Just as there is a defined set of instructional best practices that every teacher should know, there is a similar set of best practices for staff development. This set of descriptions can serve as a checklist for principals and other school leaders when designing professional development for their staffs or when asking questions of a professional development provider engaged to work with the staff. Seven elements constitute the components necessary to ensure effective and lasting professional learning. These words define effective professional development: *sustained, job-embedded, collegial, interactive, integrated, practical*, and *results-oriented* (Fogarty & Pete, 2007).

1. **Sustained:** Professional development is implemented over time, with a long-term plan and with deliberate resolve to the key components of the Common Core State Standards.
   Teachers say, "Yes, we started with the Common Core last year, but this time we are going into more depth!"

2. **Job-embedded:** Professional development works best at the worksite with designated go-to people and professional collaborators in the building to provide resources and support.
   Teachers say, "Our principal met with our collaborative team to discuss our questioning strategies with us."

3. **Collegial:** Professional development builds and supports a community of learners when there is time for conversations about how to utilize strategies in various contexts and support for assessing how things are going.
   Teachers say, "Would you mind if I came by and watched you do a cooperative task? It might help me see what they meant in the workshop."

4. **Interactive:** The principal and school leaders foster effective professional development. It invites, involves, and engages participants with rigorous modeling of classroom strategies and assessment of what worked in their classrooms.
   Teachers say, "The workshop this afternoon was over so quickly. The time just flew by because we were so busy with the authentic activities and not just sitting and listening!"

5. **Integrated:** Principals push forward with 21st century professional development methods that are varied and offer an array of methods (for example, web-based, online, text, video, and face-to-face). Online professional development resources do not replace the face-to-face model but support it to facilitate more 21st century instruction in the classroom.
   Teachers say, "This works for me, because what I miss I can get online!"

6. **Practical:** Effective school leaders know that professional development is relevant when it is aligned to the immediate concerns of the school staff. Practical professional development gives teachers what they want and need to succeed with new initiatives.

Teachers say, "This is just what I wanted. I can see how I can use it with my kids right now!"

7. **Results-oriented:** Well-designed professional development incorporates expectations of authentic implementation in the classroom (Joyce & Showers, 2002), and effective principals expect to see evidence of that learning when they go into the classroom.
Teachers say, "From our data, we conclude that we needed comprehension strategies, and there is evidence that they're working!"

School leaders can use these best practices for professional development as guides for their plans for implementing the Common Core. More specifically, three professional development elements—*sustained, job-embedded,* and *results-oriented*—become vitally important. Teachers want to know, as they face substantive changes in their day-to-day work, that the change is going to be long term and worthy of the effort required. Thus, the professional development has to be ongoing, with emphasis on depth, not breadth, and with a climate of expectations that time spent—whether for school in-service training, a conference offsite, or in the collaborative team meetings of a professional learning community—will have positive results for their classroom practice.

Two other best practices in effective professional development—*collegial* and *interactive*—reveal themselves in the actual professional development session. Time has to be provided for participants to talk about how they will transfer what they are hearing. Hearing is one thing. Learning is another. Only after teachers apply the information in their classrooms have they truly learned it.

Twenty-first century schools call for a more student-centered approach. In addition, the CCSS demand more attention be paid to higher-order thinking skills. Both of these factors mean that classroom teachers will benefit greatly from collaborations with colleagues as they increase the rigor and relevance of instruction with robust cooperative student projects. Just as cooperation is good for the classroom, it has similar effects in the staffroom. Effective leaders know how to promote collaborations. Interactive professional development models for the teachers reveal how it is easier to move from *active* to engaged learning than it is to move from *passive* to engaged learning. Both students and adult learners benefit from the collegial inquiry that carries them forward to deeper learning.

The research, according to Bruce Joyce and Beverly Showers (2002), shows that the design of professional development is the most important factor to its success. It's the design that a leader can influence in terms of how *integrated* and *practical* the training becomes. In designing the professional development plan, leaders must work out technology resources, supporting material, and online schedules. In-service training needs to focus on practical ideas that teachers can implement. Thus, when the principal looks at school-based data—summative and formative—and brings in a learning opportunity that meets the needs of his or her teachers, the staff must be clear about how the experience will help them do their job. This connection to what is needed and delivered in professional development and what the attendees are expected to do afterward in their classroom is the vital crossroads for the leader as change agent.

Design Elements of Professional Learning

Joyce and Showers (1980) note that it doesn't seem to matter where or when training is held, nor does the role of the trainer—teacher, administrator, or professor—really matter. What does matter is the *training design*. The design trumps many other factors including whether teachers organize and direct the program, although social cohesion and shared understanding do facilitate teachers' willingness to try out new ideas.

Professional development design refers to the execution of the learning objectives and showing how they are relevant to the learning goals of the school staff. Above all else, the concept of *less is more* is important (Fogarty & Pete, 2007). As Nick Saban, University of Alabama head football coach, observed on ESPN's College GameDay before the Crimson Tide's November 5, 2011, game against Louisiana State University, "See a little, see a lot. See a lot, see nothing." This idea is the standard-bearer for all professional development sessions. Go deep, rather than wide, as adult learners prefer hands-on learning that they can use immediately to survey courses that overwhelm them with inert information (Pete & Fogarty, 2010).

A principal or other instructional leader can influence the design of professional development by insisting that the training is more than a *sit and git* exercise—integrating authentic modeling and time for practice of what the teachers are expected to learn. Additionally, a coaching element is integral to the training. If a staff development provider's plan is insufficient, it's the principal's responsibility to suggest at least forty-five minutes at the end of the day to facilitate reflective conversations with peer coaching that will help to increase the chances of authentic transfer from the staffroom to classroom. Indeed, doing less to design professional development for transfer is *not* a good use of two valued resources—time and money—because it is going nowhere (Pellegrino & Hilton, 2012).

Effective professional development—training—includes the following four elements.

1. **Theory:** Research-based findings that support the concept, skill, or strategy
2. **Demonstration:** Modeling of the desired teaching behavior
3. **Practice:** Opportunity for participants to have guided practice

4. **Coaching:** A context for ongoing guidance, support, and mentoring for individuals as they engage in activities for professional revitalization

The credibility of the instructional leader is at stake every time staff members attend a professional development opportunity with him or her. Adult learners, especially classroom teachers, are practical and pragmatic learners (Fogarty & Pete, 2007). If they don't see relevance in the content they are being asked to learn, and if accountability to learn and apply the content is not required, they may be *able* participants but not necessarily *willing* participants. There must be some expectation for using the newly learned strategies. These observations provide critical insights for the field of professional development that are integral to designing successful models.

What the teacher thinks about teaching determines what the teacher does when teaching. In training teachers, therefore, the school leaders must do more than go through the motions of teaching. Teachers are likely to keep and use new strategies and concepts if they receive coaching (either expert or peer) while they are trying the new ideas in their classrooms (Joyce & Showers, 2002). Individual teaching styles and value orientations do not often affect teachers' abilities to learn from staff development. If provided a context for the new learning, teachers will be more accepting of the training. However, initial enthusiasm for training is reassuring to the organizers but has relatively little influence on learning.

Successful professional development is dependent on peer coaching, which can simply mean teachers engage in critical conversations about how and when they will implement an aspect of the training they are experiencing. Peer coaching also includes the reflective conversations teachers have after the initial training about their attempts to implement new concepts or strategies in their classroom. If this seems obvious, it should be equally obvious that teachers have to have time to plan their transfer from the staffroom to the classroom. Consider a traditional inservice in which the entire instructional staff fills the library or gym, teachers representing different grades and subject areas all sitting together. Many times this model of professional development seems to be just an entertaining departure from the stress of the classroom, rather than a purposeful collaboration of colleagues intent on taking away ideas for immediate implementation in their classroom the very next day.

According to Joyce and Showers (2002), peer coaching is a critical element in the success of professional development. Coached teachers practice new strategies more frequently and develop greater skill, use the new strategy more appropriately, exhibit greater long-term retention of knowledge about and skill with strategies, are more likely to explain new strategies with their students, and exhibit clear cognition with regard to the purposes and uses of the new strategies.

Table 2.1 captures, in a nutshell, the key points of Joyce and Showers's (2002) research on the impact of the four elements of professional development design on teachers' transfer of learning. With these data, the role of coaching is spotlighted to the point that it seems unprofessional for school leaders to plan professional learning sessions without building in the peer support.

Table 2.1: Percent of Teachers Who Will Transfer Learning to the Classroom

	Knowledge	**Skill**	**Transfer**
Theory	10 percent	5 percent	0 percent
Demonstration	30 percent	20 percent	0 percent
Practice	60 percent	60 percent	5 percent
Coaching	95 percent	95 percent	95 percent

Source: Joyce & Showers, 2002.

Seven Steps to Coaching for Transfer

An effective school leader insists that every professional development session contains time allotted during the session for critical conversations about how participants will transfer strategies into their classroom repertoire. To foster authentic application of the new learning in the classroom, Robin Fogarty and Brian Pete (2007) identify seven steps to coaching for transfer that are easily incorporated into the context of the professional development sessions—before, during, or after, as appropriate.

1. Know the theories of transfer and application.
2. Set expectations for transfer and use.
3. Model or demonstrate with real items or artifacts.
4. Note the levels of transfer from simple to complex.
5. Plot applications for the classroom.
6. Try something immediately.
7. Dialogue with a partner for ongoing support.

We clarify these steps in more depth for the principals leading the implementation of the CCSS.

Know the Theories of Transfer and Application

The prevailing theory of transfer, according to David Perkins and Gavriel Salomon (1987), is the *good shepherd theory*, which says that if we treat transfer like the shepherd treats his most-prized sheep, if we pay attention to it all of the time, there will be greater transfer from the staffroom to the classroom. For school leaders this means that *transfer* is the focus of all professional development.

Set Expectations for Transfer and Use

Instructional leaders set expectations when they set norms for everyone who attends a staff development event. One expectation might be that participants will be reporting back, not what they want to do and not what they learned but, instead, about how successful the ideas have been in their classrooms. Setting expectations reminds the staff of the goal of professional development, which is the implementation of strategies, incorporation of concepts, and changes in attitudes that teachers transfer from the staffroom to the classroom.

Model or Demonstrate With Real Items or Artifacts

Modeling a strategy or giving examples with authentic artifacts during the professional development session is a powerful way to communicate just what is expected of the teachers. Weeks after the initial session, teacher-generated artifacts displayed in the teachers' lounge model the best practice of sustained and job-embedded professional development.

Note the Levels of Transfer From Simple to Complex

Knowing and engaging in conversations about the levels of transfer increase the impact of the professional development but also make the staff more reflective professionals. The discussion about the levels of transfer from simple to complex will result in teachers trying more applications and refining current applications.

Plot Applications for the Classroom

The word *plot* is used specifically because the word *plan* is employed so often in education that teachers and leaders have become numb to its impact. School leaders want to have teachers *plotting* applications for their classroom and with their own content. The plotting should be mindful and specific—so specific that the leader, as part of setting expectations for transfer, could say, "When could I come back to your classroom and see you try that strategy?"

Try Something Immediately

The best time to implement something learned in a professional development session is as soon as possible after the event. The closer the attempts at transfer are to the original learning, the more likely it will become part of the teaching repertoire. Again, this is something that principals and other instructional leaders can share when setting expectations with the teachers for authentic use.

Dialogue With a Partner for Ongoing Support

The research on coaching reinforces the importance of colleagues talking about how and what they are going to transfer from the professional development into their classrooms (Drago-Severson, 2009; Knight, 2007). Joyce and Showers (2002) recommend peer coaches, with two teachers in the same building planning and reflecting together on their implementations of the new learnings. DuFour, DuFour, and Eaker (2002) promote professional learning communities to foster collegial conversations and reflection on instructional practices. In addition, as the staff become more familiar with the levels of transfer, they will be able to move their colleagues along with more ideas for meaningful transfer and applications.

Six Levels of Cues and Clues to Transfer

In addition to the seven steps to coaching for transfer that help teachers use the new skills and strategies appropriately and skillfully, principals will observe cues and clues that signal the depth of understanding and the comfort level of the teachers who have attended the professional development sessions and who are trying to implement the new learning in their classrooms.

Fogarty and Pete (2007) use six terms that describe the kind of authentic use the teacher exhibits in the classroom application. A teacher:

1. **Overlooks**—Does nothing
2. **Duplicates**—Copies exactly
3. **Replicates**—Tailors to needs
4. **Integrates**—Raises awareness
5. **Propagates**—Maps into different contexts
6. **Innovates**—Finds a unique application

The levels of transfer serve as starting points in the conversation about ongoing implementation. They provide the cues and clues for the principal to discuss in the coaching conference. Review the following levels, and think about what they might reveal about moving the teacher along the implementation path.

Overlooks—Does Nothing

Overlooking the opportunity to transfer an idea into classroom practices, either intentionally or unintentionally, occurs because the teacher may see no relevance and sometimes will even say, "I don't know why I'm here." Words to this effect inform the principal and let him or her know that the purpose of the workshop has not been made clear to all participants. One example of an overlooker is the teacher who learned all about cooperative learning years ago but still does not use cooperative groups in his or her classroom.

Duplicates—Copies Exactly

A duplicator reveals himself or herself when he or she says, "I won't be writing in the handout, because I want to use it just the way it is." Leaders celebrate this level of transfer, because the teachers are actually thinking about using the ideas at a foundational level. A teacher using the complex text exercise that is included in the workshop or asking to put the complex text lesson from the PowerPoint on his or her flash drive is ready, willing, and able to try something immediately.

Replicates—Tailors to Needs

The replicator changes something about the original idea to tailor it for his or her students or the content. The applications will look the same and will be in the same context of the original learning, but the teacher makes slight alterations to target the appropriate content for the students. The Spanish teacher says, "I'm going to use this strategy of comparing informational text to narrative text, but I have to write it in Spanish."

Integrates—Raises Awareness

The level of integrating is evidenced when teachers feel comfortable enough with the idea to weave it into their existing teaching repertoires. An integrator is a participant who has a raised awareness about his or her own knowledge and skill as a result of experiences in professional development activities. A common example involves the use of Bloom's Taxonomy (Bloom, 1984). Principals may hear teachers talk about the higher-order thinking skills expected in the Common Core and say, "I already try to use Bloom's Taxonomy, so this won't be that hard to do."

Propagates—Maps Into Different Contexts

To propagate means to strategize or map ideas in many different situations or contexts. This teacher sees the essence of a strategy and is able to take it and apply it fluently in many different situations beyond the context of the original learning. For example, the instructional leader notices as he or she *reads the walls* during a walkthrough that the teacher has used graphic organizers in three different subject-area exercises.

Innovates—Finds a Unique Application

This level of transfer is inspired. It diverges. It is bold and inventive. When this teacher transfers an idea from the staffroom to the classroom, professional development leaders may find it difficult to make the connection to the original learning because the teacher has applied it so uniquely. For example, a seventh-grade teacher takes the idea of graphed data and asks students to form a *human graph* in response to a survey about how much they know about learning in mathematics. The teacher's survey asks the students to rank their answers to the question, "How much do you know about how you learn math? A lot. A little. Not sure. Not much. Next to nothing." The students' responses provide revealing data that the teacher uses to determine where to focus instruction in mathematics class.

Embracing Professional Learning Communities

Teachers often lament that they haven't had common planning time. Through their work with PLCs, Richard DuFour, Rebecca DuFour, Robert Eaker, and Thomas Many have literally changed the perception of teacher collaboration and accommodations in the school schedule to enable common planning time: they have done something that was at one time considered undoable (DuFour & Eaker, 1998; DuFour, DuFour, & Eaker, 2008; DuFour, DuFour, Eaker, & Many, 2010). Yet for some schools, as they are starting a professional learning community, time for collaboration is a lingering challenge. We use an informal survey in training sessions with teachers in which we seek descriptions of their PLC. Some teachers report that PLCs are sometimes like a junior high school dance in the gym. Everything is set up with the music, lights, punch, and cookies yet the girls are lined up on one side of the gym, and the boys are hanging together on the other side. An effective school leader knows that the collaborative teams in his or her school need structure, guidance, and ongoing support. He wants to make sure that all the team members know how to dance.

The Definition of PLCs

Since the 1990s, schools throughout the United States have been experiencing a quiet revolution called the *professional learning community*. The PLC is:

> an ongoing process in which educators work collaboratively in recurring cycles of collective inquiry and action research to achieve better results for the students they serve. Professional learning communities operate under the assumption that the key to improved learning for students is continuous job-embedded learning for educators. (DuFour et al., 2010, p. 11)

"Whatever it takes" is the pledge that guides practices in a PLC. Teachers are organized into collaborative teams as an extended opportunity to foster learning among colleagues. PLCs focus on three big ideas: (1) student learning, (2) teacher collaboration, and (3) results (DuFour et al., 2008; DuFour et al., 2010).

ATTRIBUTES OF PROFESSIONAL LEARNING COMMUNITIES

Big Idea 1: A Focus on Student Learning

- What do we want each student to learn?

- How will we know when each student has learned it?

- How will we respond when a student experiences difficulty in learning?

- How will we use timely, directive intervention rather than remediation?

Big Idea 2: A Focus on Teacher Collaboration

- How will we design professional dialogue that transforms a school into a PLC?

- How will we remove barriers to successful collaborations?

Big Idea 3: A Focus on Results

- How will we use data results to avoid being data rich but information poor?

- How will we determine the progress we have made on goals that are important to us?

Visit www.allthingsplc.info for PLC resources.

Source: DuFour et al., 2008; DuFour et al., 2010.

The Mission of PLCs

The true mission of the PLC bears repeating. It is captured simply in four critical questions about student success. These questions establish the foundation for the work of collaborative planning teams in a professional learning community (DuFour et al., 2008).

1. What do we want our students to learn?
2. How will we know when they have learned it?
3. How will we respond when some students don't learn?
4. How will we extend and enrich the learning for students who are already proficient?

These questions provide a foundation for leaders as they guide implementation of the CCSS.

- **"What do we want our students to learn?"** This question is all about the Common Core State Standards. These standards delineate content and learning processes across the grade levels. What they don't do is expand on how to design curriculum and instruction to deliver this content. Decisions about the content change as students come to school with skills already learned; for example, some students know how to read before kindergarten or first grade. Other decisions relate to forms of delivery for content like print or digital. Questions arise about how much instructional time should be spent on what is considered traditional content, such as spelling. This beginning step in the PLC mission is where educators look for guidance from the Common Core State Standards. School staffs compare and contrast the standards they have been using to the Common Core and make the needed adjustments in their curriculum. A theme in the Common Core is the value of teaching the content but also the rigorous process. What we want students to know is best described in terms of content. What we want students to be able to do is best answered by focusing on learning process skills—collaborating, thinking critically, reasoning, and communicating in speaking and writing.

- **"How will we know when they have learned it?"** This question leads directly to the focus on continuous formative assessments to supplement data from summative assessments. Leaders help teachers gather and analyze assessment data and make decisions about the best kind of instruction to provide based on the data. Responding to this question means ensuring that assessments are aligned with what has been taught and provide the valued student feedback about how things are going. Assessments, formative and summative, have always been a part of the teaching and learning equation, but with the advent of the Common Core, the need for constant and continual feedback is critical because of the shift toward more rigor.

- **"How will we respond when some students don't learn?"** and **"How will we extend and enrich the learning for students who are already proficient?"** These two questions are about differentiating instruction for learners who are developing, struggling, or advanced, as well as English learners and students with special needs. It is how teachers respond to students' talents and needs. What teachers do when students don't know the information or when they already know the information is known as *differentiated instruction* (Fogarty & Pete, 2011). Changing something—content, process, strategy, or product—to address the talents and needs of students is why data are collected, analyzed, and interpreted. Data results guide teachers in making decisions about planning differentiated instruction. Thus, it behooves the principal or school leader to begin or continue to concentrate efforts on differentiated instruction with implementation of the CCSS.

High-Functioning Collaborative Teams in a PLC

Collaborative teams comprised of creative, experienced, and novice teachers functioning in the school's PLC value the professional conversations that they have about data-driven decisions focused on student success. Every collaborative team meeting is, in essence, a prime opportunity for members to share with each other. Sometimes, one of the members "teaches" an instructional strategy for the differentiated classroom or shares an insight about students or data. There are also occasions when the time is used to write common assessments or to interact with each other, using an engaging classroom strategy on a current topic of interest.

The topics covered, issues resolved, and the decisions made in collaborative team meetings are important to ensure student achievement in the school. Yet, when teachers are given the chance during the course of the meeting to experience an appropriate classroom strategy and to plan its implementation, the PLC reaches a whole new level of influence. It is this expectation of transfer from the collaborative team meetings to the classrooms that the school principal, as instructional leader, can facilitate through modeling while conducting his or her own staff meetings.

The structure of the PLC allows for sustained and job-embedded professional development. In collaborative teams, teachers can support each other and provide momentum to understand and implement the latest instructional initiatives. Reflective dialogues and professional conversations are at the heart of the teams' work. The instructional leader can guide these interactions with expectations of reflective practices by suggesting questions for the teams to discuss in their sessions.

Teachers in collaborative teams discover that as the individuals closest to the problems, they are more likely to have solutions to the problems (Deming, 2000). Through their commitment to professional sharing, they become empowered to work together and achieve goals.

Looking Back

A brief look back at this chapter reveals a comprehensive discussion of professional development support for teachers, as they work to fully implement the CCSS. From the initial orientation for staff as well as grade-level and department teams, the leader plans, audits, elicits, and often administers the supporting options for teachers. In addition, leaders monitor the transfer of learning as they observe teachers, looking for practices that support authentic implementation. They also look for signs of the levels of transfer that are observable through teacher and student behaviors, artifacts, and other evidences of learning. Professional development, the focus of this chapter, is the lynchpin for long-term implementation and institutionalization of new practices in the classrooms.

Discussion Questions

The discussion questions are for collaborative, grade-level, or department teams or even just two colleagues working together or with a principal as part of a staff meeting to discuss this chapter as part of a book study or as a stand-alone chapter with good information and examples for rigorous and relevant learning. There is nothing as powerful as reflective conversation among professionals.

1. To discover the history of a strategy in your repertoire, think about one that you learned as a teacher, and see if you can trace its roots, how it was first presented, how it changed as you used it, and how you changed as you used it. Do you find that teachers with whom you are working are using this or a comparable strategy? What have you observed about their development in the use of the strategy?

2. When considering dialogue with a colleague about something new he or she is using in the classroom, identify what you consider to be more important: the conversation before the event or the one after. Explain how the conversations would likely differ.

3. Pinpoint a specific shortcoming of the professional development that your teachers have experienced over the years. How could you overcome this shortcoming through a dialogue with the provider?

4. How might you use the list of seven best features of professional development (page 48) to improve the offerings in your school or district?

Takeaways

In a final look back, consider the following takeaways for this chapter. These are just some of the learnings that will benefit you as you support, observe, and evaluate great instruction.

- How and when principals and school leaders can "model the model" of engaged learning

- Transfer and authentic implementation in the classroom as the goal of all professional development

- The potential and power of functioning PLCs

CHAPTER 3

The Shift in Instruction

Attaining Rigor and Real-World Relevance

It might be easier to define rigor by noting what it is not: Rigor is not a synonym for "harder," and it does not mean moving first-grade curriculum into kindergarten, or algebra into the seventh grade . . . Rigor means teaching and learning things more thoroughly—more deeply.

—Nancy Flanagan

According to Madeline Hunter, "Teachers make 1,500 decisions in a day. Some are on-your-seat decisions and some are on-your-feet decisions. On-your-seat decisions are during the quiet, thoughtful times of the day, when the students are gone, while on-your-feet decisions are made in the heat of the action all day long. . . . In terms of instructional decision making, the tradition of covering your content is much like taking a passenger to the airport. You rush around and get to the airport on time, but you left the passenger at home."

Her final question was the clincher. "Think about it. When you got to the end of the textbook, did all of the kids come with you?" (Hunter & Russel, 1994)

This chapter is about more rigorous and more relevant learning and what leaders will be looking for in Common Core classrooms. The instruction is deeper, the pace is slower, and the frequent and intentional interactions of students in reading, writing, speaking, and listening are integral to the teaching and learning process. As Sandra Day O'Connor (2013) said in her keynote address in Chicago at the 2013 ASCD conference: "Teach them to read fast and to write well!"

A High Standard of Learning

School leaders are in charge of changing classroom instructional practices. They lead plans to align the curriculum to the CCSS ELA/literacy and mathematics. Additionally, they set direction for the professional development program, sustain coaching conversations that support it, and evaluate the results of professional development on student achievement. Although leaders are responsible for overseeing and monitoring instructional effectiveness, they alone cannot ensure that the Common Core vision of rigor and real-world relevance becomes a reality. Teachers must play a premier role in instructional decision making for the implementation of the CCSS.

Teachers set the expectations—academic, social, and behavioral—for student learning in their classrooms. If the teacher's goals are mediocre, the students' effort will mirror that mediocrity. On the other hand, when the teacher sets the bar high and follows through with robust learning tasks, students rise to the occasion. Over time, students understand that less than their personal best is just not good enough.

Research strongly supports the contention that teachers make *the* difference not *a* difference in the learning journey of every child (Brophy, 2006; Brophy & Good, 1986; Good, 2010). Professional teachers know the impact they have on student learning; consequently, they often welcome feedback from the trained eye and the coaching voice of the school leaders. Teachers understand that ultimately they bear the burden of responsibility to reach and teach every student in their classrooms, and they want the seasoned advice of their leaders. In this context, we focus on instructional changes that derive from the CCSS.

Technology Use and Integration

Part and parcel of effective instruction in every classroom is the role technology plays in the teaching and learning process. Excellence in 21st century instruction depends on leaders and teachers integrating technology-rich digital tools in the classroom.

Digital literacy can be woven seamlessly into classroom instruction and multidisciplinary projects. For gathering data, students learn how to go online, browse topics, and analyze reading material for bias. They learn to use digital tools to create a blog, a PowerPoint presentation, a webpage, or a digital video to communicate their ideas. Digital tools for students are readily available at sites like ReadWriteThink (www.read writethink.org) and ClassTools (www.classtools.net). Online journals and portfolios provide an opportunity for students to reflect on what they are learning through the many dimensions of inquiry learning.

These technologies not only frame the students' in-school learning but also serve as a means to an end to their real-world learning. Digital literacy is as integral to college and career readiness as are traditional literacy and thinking skills. Technology can be integrated into all aspects of instruction; effective use of technology supports the shift to rigor and real-world relevance that the CCSS require.

High-Yield Instructional Strategies

Four instructional strategies warrant the spotlight as leaders and teachers consider the best ways to implement the CCSS. Leaders can reference these examples of sound and effective instruction as they plan professional development opportunities, support collaborative teams, conduct classroom observations, and provide coaching and feedback to teachers. Consistent with achieving the dual goals of academic rigor and real-world relevance in the instructional area, the four strategies are the following.

1. **Explicit instruction of thinking skills** empowers students' learning across the disciplines (Bellanca, Fogarty, & Pete, 2012).

2. **Close reading of text** involves teachers in designing text-dependent tasks that require students to rigorously analyze both narrative and informational text (Monk, 2003; Piercy, 2011).

3. **Concept-rich mathematics instruction** focuses on the big ideas in mathematics rather than the more traditional skills-based model (Ben-Hur, 2006).

4. **Inquiry learning** is an umbrella term that includes student-centered and student-directed models of learning: problem-based, project-based, service learning, case studies, and thematic instruction (Bellanca, 2010; Fogarty, 1997).

These four instructional practices provide the grounding students need to be prepared to address the unfamiliar complex problems they will undoubtedly face in the future. Informed teachers use these approaches to provide students with tools to confront problems with a critical eye, a creative mind, and a disposition of confidence. In these lessons, students become practiced in the complex behaviors they will be using throughout their college years and their chosen and changing careers. The mission of school leaders is to achieve this goal for *all* students and provide teachers with the support and resources they need to accomplish the goal.

Explicit Instruction of Thinking Skills

With school improvement efforts throughout the United States, the concept of *explicit instruction of thinking skills* is re-emerging as a viable and necessary approach to sound instruction. While direct instruction has never completely receded from the classroom scene, the focus is now clearly on the concept of *explicitness*—instruction that provides students with a solid platform for learning specific skills and strategies, including how to think before they perform the tasks independently. Explicit instruction is the opposite of the all-too-common *assign and assess* teaching practice. School leaders know that practice is not and never has been enough to ensure that all students succeed. Students need explicit instruction in thinking processes for mastery of skills and concepts that comprise the CCSS.

The three-phase explicit instruction of thinking skills model combines direct instruction with the gradual release of responsibility model of instruction, mirroring the "I do, we do, you do" mantra (Bellanca et al., 2012). Lev Vygotsky, an icon of cognitive psychology, developed the zone of proximal development theory (Cole, 1978). This theory is a foundation for the gradual release of responsibility model of instruction. Instructional leaders and teachers are well aware of the power of appropriately guided instruction this model defines. The zone of proximal development theory offers a developmental philosophy that educators often voice in the instructional mantra "I do, we do, you do" (Fisher & Frey, 2007; Maeirs, 2009). Throughout this book, we demonstrate the link between the explicit instruction of thinking skills and the Common Core State Standards' focus on what students will be able to do and understand. Based on the precedent of this historical landscape, the discussion of the three-phase model for explicit instruction of thinking skills is fully described for school leaders as a best practice to initiate, implement, and institutionalize the Common Core State Standards (Fullan, 2001).

The three phases comprise the complete lesson in which *process* (a thinking skill) becomes the content. These are explicit teaching elements that instructional leaders look for in their work with teachers. The three phases are the following.

- **Phase I: The Talk-Through**—Teacher-led explicit modeling of the skill
- **Phase II: The Walk-Through**—Teacher-guided student application of the skill
- **Phase III: The Drive-Through**—Student use of the skill independently in a Common Core performance task

Teacher-directed or guided inquiry of step-by-step instruction is an essential methodology for effective classroom instruction. Additionally, at the same time, the gradual release of responsibility is the means to the goal. After all, the end goal is that students become productive consumers and producers of information and that they are able to continue to learn on their own throughout their lives.

Phase I: The Talk-Through—Explicit Teaching Lesson

In this initial phase, the collaborative teams (grade level or department) review the standards required and their student achievement data with school leaders. After specifically analyzing the disaggregated data of the subskills or by utilizing the sample performance tasks in the CCSS, the teams select several thinking skills that seem particularly problematic for their students. For example, deficit areas often include comprehension skills—making inferences, determining central themes or main ideas, or problem solving and doing statistical analysis.

Once a team decides on a thinking skill to thread through its specific disciplines, the teachers develop and present a generic lesson on the target thinking skill—*analysis*, for example. Thinking is the subject of this lesson, and the skill of analysis is the topic. For example, an eighth-grade team uses its CCSS-based curriculum to make the decision to target the skill of *analysis*. Table 3.1 (page 66) shows the interrelatedness of Reading and Writing standards that feature analysis. This table illustrates the range of choices available to the team to target the skill of analysis in reading and writing.

As teachers conduct the generic lesson on analysis, they do a direct, step-by-step instructional *talk-aloud* to clarify the thinking that is occurring in each step of the analysis activity. More specifically, the explicit teaching phase includes essential elements that comprise the teacher-led lesson. These elements include a motivational mindset, a description, an order of operations, an instructional strategy, an assessment, and a metacognitive reflection (see figure 3.1, page 67). See the reproducible "Phase I: The Talk-Through—Explicit Teaching Lesson" (page 90) for a lesson template to use with teachers.

Phase II: The Walk-Through—Classroom Application Lesson

Next, leaders support teachers and teacher teams as they target standards-based classroom topics within their subject matter and give students authentic practice in applying the explicit thinking skill. Teachers will use the target thinking skill at every opportunity to give students repeated practice in using the skill. At the same time, leaders need to be aware of the level of support that teachers need as they proceed to phase II of the explicit instruction model. Leaders may observe an application lesson to see how well students are applying the higher-level thinking skills and provide valued feedback to the teacher.

Students often need repeated practices using the skill with regular classroom content. In addition, these practice lessons are usually teacher guided as the students are learning to become more competent with their applications of the target thinking skill. The purpose of phase II is teacher guidance—supporting students in using the targeted skill or strategy. Teachers will find many opportunities to have students apply the skill of analysis across the curriculum. In history, students may analyze the point of view of the parties considering waging war; in literature, they may analyze the point of view of two characters; or in health, they may analyze the point of view of the patient and the research firm. The goal is to have students effectively apply the skill of *analysis* in various settings within a subject area and, in turn, to use this explicitly taught skill with effectiveness across the disciplines.

Table 3.1: Analysis in Reading and Writing Standards, Grade 8

Anchor Standards	Domain	Grade-Level Standard
CCRA.R.3: Analyze how and why individuals, events, and ideas develop and interact over the course of a text.	Key Ideas and Details	**RL.8.3:** Analyze how particular lines of dialogue or incidents in a story or drama propel the action, reveal aspects of a character, or provoke a decision. **RI.8.3:** Analyze how a text makes connections between individuals, ideas, or events (for example, through comparisons, analogies, or categories).
CCRA.R.5: Analyze the structure of texts, including how specific sentences, paragraphs, and larger portions of the text (for example, a section, chapter, scene, or stanza) related to each other and the whole. **CCRA.R.6:** Assess how point of view or purpose shapes the content and style of a text.	Craft and Structure	**RL.8.5:** Compare and contrast the structure of two or more texts and analyze how the differing structure of each text contributes to its meaning and style. **RI.8.5:** Analyze in detail the structure of a specific paragraph in a text, including the role of particular sentences in developing and refining a concept. **RL.8.6:** Analyze how differences in the points of view of the characters and the audience or reader (for example, created through the use of dramatic irony) create such effects as suspense or humor. **RI.8.6:** Determine an author's point of view or purpose in a text and analyze how the author acknowledges and responds to conflicting evidence or viewpoints.
CCRA.R.9: Analyze how two or more texts address similar themes or topics in order to build knowledge or to compare the approaches the authors take.	Integration of Knowledge and Ideas	**RL.8.9:** Analyze how a modern work of fiction draws on themes, patterns of events, or character types from myths, traditional stories, or religious works such as the Bible, including describing how the material is rendered new. **RI.8.9:** Analyze a case in which two or more texts provide conflicting information on the same topic and identify where the texts disagree on matters of fact or interpretation.
CCRA.W.9: Draw evidence from literary or informational texts to support analysis, reflection, and research.	Research to Build and Present Knowledge	**W.8.9:** Draw evidence from literary or informational texts to support analysis, reflection, and research. a. Apply grade 8 Reading standards to literature (for example, RL.8.9). b. Apply grade 8 Reading standards to literacy nonfiction (for example, RI.8.8).

Source: Adapted from NGA & CCSSO, 2010b, pp. 35, 36, 37, 39, 41, and 44.

Target thinking skill: Analysis

1. **Motivational mindset:** The teacher provides a hook or a student motivator, an engaging brain-compatible strategy that arouses interest and curiosity about the learning. For example, note the parts of the flag that comprise the whole: pole, fabric, stars, stripes, colors, and design.

2. **Description:** The class has a discussion that examines and explains the target thinking skill in detail and with synonyms and phrases as examples that can be dissected or disassembled.

3. **Order of operations:** The teacher then delineates the actual mental processing that occurs when using the target thinking skill using the acronym PART:

   P—Preview the whole situation

   A—Assess the individual parts

   R—Reorganize the parts by similarities and differences

   T—Turn analysis into summary or synthesis of selection

4. **Instructional strategy:** Teachers then present a user-friendly, high-energy, mindfully engaging activity that addresses the thinking skill explicitly as the content of the lesson; for example, apply PART to a kitchen appliance.

5. **Assessment:** The teacher does an evaluation exercise to determine the level and quality of understanding of the thinking skill. For example, check each element of PART to see if the student followed the process for analyzing in the task. Were you able to do the series of steps efficiently?

6. **Metacognitive reflection:** The class then takes a deliberate look back on the learning that has occurred and considers possible applications for the future; for example, the teacher might ask, "How might you use the skill of analysis when editing your first draft essay?"

Figure 3.1: Elements of the Talk-Through.

*Visit **go.solution-tree.com/leadership** for a reproducible version of this figure.*

Thinking skills permeate the Common Core. Consequently, it is neither practical nor possible to target all the thinking skills individually. Teacher teams need to select the high-frequency thinking skills—evaluating, hypothesizing, clarifying, and reasoning—their students most need. This is a data-driven decision the teams must make. Once the teams select the skills, teach them explicitly, and apply them frequently and with fidelity, students begin to grow in their abilities as thinkers. In turn, they begin to have more confidence in themselves as students who can be successful.

The lesson structure for phase II—the Walk-Through—has four elements as shown in figure 3.2.

Target thinking skill: _____

1. Define the target thinking skill.

2. Establish a motivational mindset.

3. Provide a standards-based content lesson that requires application of the target thinking skill.

4. Provide closure through an assessment or reflection activity.

Figure 3.2: Elements of the Walk-Through.

*Visit **go.solution-tree.com/leadership** for a reproducible version of this figure.*

See the reproducible "Phase II: The Walk-Through—Classroom Application Lesson" (page 91) for a lesson template to use with teachers.

Phase III: The Drive-Through—Common Core Performance Task Lesson

Gradually, the teacher steps back to provide opportunities for students to practice the skill independently with relevant material that is integral to the curriculum. This is the "you do" aspect of the gradual release of responsibility model—the step that fosters student mastery. As students become proficient with the targeted thinking skill, the skill becomes a skill for life lessons as well as for classroom lessons in all disciplines.

In phase III, students are now ready to try their hand at performance tasks such as those in appendix B of the CCSS (NGA & CCSSO, 2010d). This is the final phase in which the students are behind the wheel and ready to drive on their own. As teachers move students into this phase, leaders need to be particularly attentive in monitoring and providing supportive feedback to the teachers. Sometimes teachers are reluctant to step back and let the students struggle a bit. However, this is exactly how they become more self-directed and independent as thinkers and problem solvers. Leaders who effectively present the model in professional development sessions provide the guidance and support teachers may need as they develop skill in applying a new lesson structure.

The sample performance tasks in the Common Core ELA/literacy (NGA & CCSSO, 2010d) are models teachers can use to create their own tasks based on content they are using in their classrooms. Figure 3.3 (page 70) presents sample performance tasks and associated Common Core standards for the target thinking skill analysis. The examples, based on middle school–level performance tasks, exemplify the robust and rigorous analysis students must be able to do as they compare various texts. The examples are quite typical of the tasks in the Common Core that focus on reading informational and narrative text as well as analyzing excerpts in the same genre.

Teachers guide the first attempts at the performance tasks with appropriate step-by-step scaffolding. As this process of addressing actual performance unfolds, students take on more and more of the responsibility to complete these tasks on their own. This is an area in which leaders may need to remind teachers to overcome the *test-prep syndrome*—overprompting students with sample test questions—that can potentially take over these performances and outweigh the intent of developing self-reliant learners. The desired outcome is that students become competent with the layered rigor of these tasks and eventually become proficient thinkers, speakers, and writers for independent performances that are rich and real-world relevant.

Starting with the metacognitive Talk-Through of a targeted learning skill in an explicit teaching lesson, following it with a Walk-Through of relevant and real applications of the skill within subject-matter content, and, finally, applying the skill in a Drive-Through of complex real-world CCSS performance tasks, students become comfortable and confident. They rise to the demands of the task with the skillfulness necessary for college and careers. Figure 3.4 (page 71) shows the elements in phase III of the explicit instruction model.

See the reproducible "Phase III: The Drive-Through—Common Core Performance Task Lesson" (page 92) for a lesson template to use with teachers.

The three-phase model for explicit teaching enables teachers to guide their students toward independent learning. To be effective, teachers should address the complete cycle. Phase I—the Talk-Through—is an explicit teacher-directed lesson that focuses on the thinking skill as the content; the teacher then moves to multiple applications of the thinking skill with classroom content. In phase II—the Walk-Through—the teacher guides students as they use the skill purposefully. Lastly, for phase III—the Drive-Through—students independently manage their work, showing evidence using the skill effectively. All three phases are integral to the acquisition and application of the thinking skill for student mastery. In turn, it is a process that is often repeated as various thinking skills are addressed explicitly.

CCRA.R.9: Analyze how two or more texts address similar themes or topics in order to build knowledge or to compare the approaches the authors take.

RL.7.9: Compare and contrast a fictional portrayal of a time, place, or character and a historical account of the same period as a means of understanding how authors of fiction use or alter history.

Sample performance task, grade 7: Students compare and contrast Laurence Yep's fictional portrayal of Chinese immigrants in San Francisco at the turn of the 20th century in *Dragonwings* to historical accounts of the same period. For example, they use materials detailing the 1906 San Francisco earthquake in order to glean a deeper understanding of how authors use or alter historical sources to create a sense of time and place as well as make the fictional characters lifelike and real.

CCRA.R.3: Analyze how and why individuals, events, and ideas develop and interact over the course of a text.

RI.6.3: Analyze in detail how a key individual, event, or idea is introduced, illustrated, or elaborated in a text (for example, through examples or anecdotes).

Sample performance task, grade 6: Students analyze in detail how the early years of Harriet Tubman (as author Ann Petry relates) contributed to her later becoming a conductor on the Underground Railroad, attending to how the author introduces, illustrates, and elaborates on the events in Tubman's life.

Figure 3.3: Sample CCSS performance tasks for analysis.

Source: NGA & CCSSO, 2010d, pp. 35, 37, 39, 89, and 93.

Close Reading of Text

The Common Core ELA/literacy contain many examples of tasks that require close reading—for example, read closely to determine what the text says, analyze the structure of texts, cite textual evidence to support the author's point of view, evaluate argumentative or opinion writing, and demonstrate understanding of figurative language. Close reading (Piercy, 2011) is a distinctively rigorous reading strategy that is integral to the transition to and teaching within the Common Core. In fact, this is a prime skill for leaders to model and coach for all staff as they learn how to shift from covering the content to deep analysis and close reading of selected excerpts and less overall content. The emphasis on close reading in the CCSS ELA/literacy is clearly expressed in anchor standard ten (CCRA.R.10): "Read and comprehend complex literary and informational texts independently and proficiently" (NGA & CCSSO, 2010b, p. 10). Other standards specify that students are expected to gather evidence to support their responses. In these cases, close reading means text-dependent

Target thinking skill: _____

1. Define the target thinking skill.

2. Guide student practice in a standards-based content lesson that requires application of the target thinking skill.

3. Allow for independent performance of skill.

4. Ensure evidence of student learning.

Figure 3.4: Elements of the Drive-Through.

*Visit **go.solution-tree.com/leadership** for a reproducible version of this figure.*

reading or analytical reading that may require text-to-text analysis, linking the new information to complementary knowledge (Anderson, 1977; Piaget, 1926/2011), as opposed to text-to-self schema, comparing to personal experiences, which is more commonly evidenced in student work and in lower-level assessment questions.

Close reading enables students to analyze texts. Developing this skill requires explicit instruction. The CCSS use several terms that specify the need for students to read closely in order to analyze the literary and informational texts they are using. The thinking skill analysis is one that students will apply in a variety of contexts, including standards from the Speaking and Listening strand and Language strand (see examples in table 3.2, page 72).

Because students are often not well-schooled in the sophisticated technique of close analytical reading with text-based evidence, teachers need to concentrate instruction to prepare students to read closely for text references to support their responses and extend comprehension. In collaborative team meetings, school leaders can demonstrate close-reading strategies and coach teachers so they can see how the approach can be used across all subject areas. Remember, the hallmark of the Common Core is its call for teachers' shared responsibility for students' development of literacy in English language arts, history and social studies, science, mathematics, and technical subjects in kindergarten through grade 12.

Close reading involves four features that scaffold students in the process. These are similar to the gradual release of responsibility model we describe in the explicit instruction model (see pages 63–70). This scaffolding leads students to become critical consumers of complex text. Additionally, it is a perfect lesson for teachers to actually try themselves with the guidance of an instructional leader. The four components of a close-reading lesson are the following (Monk, 2003).

Table 3.2: Analysis in Speaking and Listening Standards and Language Standards, Grade 4

Anchor Standards	Domain	Grade-Level Standard
CCRA.SL.6: Adapt speech to a variety of contexts and communicative tasks, demonstrating command of formal English when indicated or appropriate.	Presentation of Knowledge and Ideas	**SL.4.6:** Differentiate between contexts that call for formal English (for example, presenting ideas) and situations where informal discourse is appropriate (for example, small-group discussion); use formal English when appropriate to task and situation. (See grade 4 Language standards for specific expectations.)
CCRA.L.4: Determine or clarify the meaning of unknown and multiple-meaning words and phrases by using context clues, analyzing meaningful word parts, and consulting general and specialized reference materials, as appropriate.	Vocabulary Acquisition and Use	**L.4.4:** Determine or clarify the meaning of unknown and multiple-meaning words and phrases based on grade 4 reading and content, choosing flexibly from a range of strategies. a. Use context (for example, definitions, examples, or restatements in text) as a clue to the meaning of a word or phrase. b. Use common, grade-appropriate Greek and Latin affixes and roots as clues to the meaning of a word (for example, *telegraph*, *photograph*, and *autograph*). c. Consult reference materials (for example, dictionaries, glossaries, and thesauruses), both print and digital, to find the pronunciation and determine or clarify the precise meaning of key words and phrases.

Source: Adapted from NGA & CCSSO, 2010b, pp. 22, 24, 25, and 29.

1. Selected reading excerpt
2. Text-dependent questions
3. Instructional tasks aligned to the questions
4. Appropriate task assessment

Selected Reading Excerpt

Teachers should select a variety of excerpts from various texts across subject areas and across a range of complexity levels. Working together in their collaborative grade-level or department teams with direction from the school leaders, teachers can explore aspects of texts that require students to read closely and the kinds of instructional support students need as they develop this skill. For students to learn the technique and then apply it with know-how and confidence takes time and effort on their part. As the process becomes a part of best practices in the classroom instructional arena, the instructional leader has a critical role in supporting the work of teachers and in communicating the expectations and accountability for evidence of student growth and development in tackling complex text.

Text-Dependent Questions

Teachers have access to many resources from which they can take excerpts to provide students with practice in responding to text-dependent questions as part of helping them learn how to read texts closely. The Common Core ELA performance text exemplar based on the preamble and First Amendment to the U.S. Constitution is an example of a primary source teachers can use for student close reading and analysis of complex text (see NGA & CCSSO, 2010d, p. 93).

Preamble:

We the People of the United States, in Order to form a more perfect Union, establish Justice, insure domestic Tranquility, provide for the common defence, promote the general Welfare, and secure the Blessings of Liberty to ourselves and our Posterity, do ordain and establish this Constitution of the United States of America. (U.S. Const. pmbl.)

First Amendment:

Congress shall make no law respecting the establishment of religion, or prohibiting the free exercise thereof; or abridging the freedom of speech, or of the press; or the right of people peaceably to assemble, and to petition the Government for a redress of grievances. (U.S. Const. amend. I)

The first and most important element of close reading is to understand the difference between *text-dependent questions* and *non-text-dependent questions*. An example of a text-dependent question is, Why did the Founding Fathers use the words "to ourselves and our Posterity" in reference to the preamble to the Constitution? On the other hand, a non-text-dependent question is, How does the preamble relate to a pledge you have made in your personal life? The text-dependent question directs the reader to the text to examine the context of the phrase "and our Posterity," in order to discern the reason for the authors' word choice. On the other hand, the non-text-dependent question references a connection to the reader's personal situation and does not dictate an analysis of the text but rather a simple understanding of the text. This distinction is a critical piece of knowledge that exemplary teachers model in classrooms by shifting their questions for more text-dependent responses. The school leadership should be prepared to work closely with teachers providing practice and coaching to enable teachers to make the transition to this type of questioning. Text-dependent questioning is a big shift from questioning practices centered on students' personal connections and interpretations of text.

Instructional Tasks Aligned to the Questions

To accommodate this shift in practice, teachers arrange instructional tasks in a memory-friendly way, such as using a variation of an acronym as we have done with the phrase "Répondez s'il vous plaît" (RSVP) or "Please respond" to which we have added another letter (E) for expression, to complete the analysis process.

> **R:** Reading task
>
> **S:** Syntax and structure task
>
> **V:** Vocabulary task
>
> **P:** Point of view and author's purpose task
>
> **E:** Expressive writing task

See figure 3.5 for sample instructional tasks for close reading based on the U.S. Constitution.

Once students have completed the analytical tasks, in their effort to understand more deeply what the author has presented, an assessment of the task is appropriate. This affirms that the students do indeed have a deeper understanding.

Appropriate Task Assessment

Appropriate assessment tasks might be as simple as a quiz that calls for a reasoned and logical answer about the gist of the text, or a quoted excerpt that sums up the message, or even an oral explanation of the text between two students or with the teacher. It's just that final accountability piece that provides structure for the stated expectations.

See figure 3.6 (page 77) for sample appropriate task assessments for close reading based on the U.S. Constitution.

The assessment is that closure piece that signifies to the students that their understanding of how to do close reading of text to extract the meaning is a skill that matters. A familiar saying in education is "What's counted, counts!" That is the rationale for assessment of this kind, yet, the feedback it provides to teachers is invaluable as they plan their next lessons.

Reading Task

Students read the passage silently and then follow along as the teacher reads the passage aloud. Students then reread particular passages in response to questions that require close examination of the text.

Example

A teacher might ask, "Why did the Founding Fathers use the words 'to petition the Government for a redress of grievances' in the First Amendment?"

First Amendment:

"Congress shall make no law respecting the establishment of religion, or prohibiting the free exercise thereof; or abridging the freedom of speech, or of the press; or the right of people peaceably to assemble, and to petition the Government for a redress of grievances" (U.S. Const. amend. I).

Sentence Syntax Task

Teachers must deconstruct the syntax or construction of complex sentences and discuss the meaning for students to become proficient at comprehending highly complex text. This teacher-directed process of analyzing and taking apart the components and structure of a troubling sentence prepares students with the necessary skills to do this as an independent and critical reader.

Example

"Congress shall make no law respecting the establishment of religion, or prohibiting the free exercise thereof" (U.S. Const. amend. I).

Students may need help in referencing or relating the last phrase, "or prohibiting the free exercise thereof," to the idea of the law respecting the establishment of religion as they may not have seen that archaic phrasing and syntax.

Vocabulary Task

Teachers underline, describe, and define words that cannot be determined from the context. The importance of a robust vocabulary requires that highly abstract words be discussed thoroughly, with modeling and strategies for student growth and development in this critical area of literacy.

Example

In the preamble, the teacher underlines the words tranquility, ordain, and posterity for explicit teaching.

Figure 3.5: Sample RSVPE instructional tasks for close reading. Continued→

Visit go.solution-tree.com/leadership for a reproducible version of this figure.

"We the People of the United States, in Order to form a more perfect Union, establish Justice, insure domestic Tranquility, provide for the common defence, promote the general Welfare, and secure the Blessings of Liberty to ourselves and our Posterity, do ordain and establish this Constitution of the United States of America" (U.S. Const. pmbl.).

Oral Interpretation Task

Discussion often calls for students to reread the passage of the text in order to dissect the meaning, and at the same time, they improve their fluency in reading difficult text. Specific activities such as highlighting the author's interpretation of a certain passage for examination provide students with the needed attention about how to handle complex text.

Example

Students may choral read the preamble with a partner to emphasize the natural phrasing and cadence of the language in it.

"We the People of the United States, in Order to form a more perfect Union, establish Justice, insure domestic Tranquility, provide for the common defence, promote the general Welfare, and secure the Blessings of Liberty to ourselves and our Posterity, do ordain and establish this Constitution of the United States of America" (U.S. Const. pmbl.).

Expressive Writing Task

Students need practice in explaining the meaning of complex text, rephrasing, paraphrasing, and clarifying what they are taking away from the passage. Exercises that require paragraphs, bullet points, analogies, and metaphors are tools that teachers might assign as students become competent producers of expressive text. Of course in these exercises, there is always the caveat that students must reference the text to support their position.

Example

Students can write an analogy using the following wording to accentuate the meaning of the preamble to the Constitution.

"The preamble is like _____ because both _____."

One example might be, "The preamble is like an appetizer because both _____."

High-Tech Traditional Assessment

Give students the choice to present a paraphrased text message of the preamble or a tweet of 140 characters.

Traditional Assessment

Ask students to write a paragraph illustrating their paraphrased account of the intent of the Founding Fathers.

Electronic or Folder Portfolio Assessment

Have students create a webpage that depicts their understanding of the preamble and what is meant by "We the People" then and now.

Performance Assessment

Have students develop a PowerPoint presentation that demonstrates the preamble then and now.

Figure 3.6: Sample appropriate task assessments for close reading.

Visit **go.solution-tree.com/leadership** *for a reproducible version of this figure.*

Concept-Rich Mathematics Instruction

The concept-rich mathematics of the CCSS consist of conceptual frames threaded across grades K–12 emphasizing authentic problem solving with progressively increasing complexity. These standards define what students should understand and be able to do in their study of mathematics. NGA and CCSSO (2010e) explain:

> Asking a student to understand something means asking a teacher to assess whether the student has understood it. One hallmark of mathematical understanding is the ability to justify, in a way appropriate to the student's mathematical maturity, why a particular mathematical statement is true or where a mathematical rule comes from. (p. 4)

This more complex approach to teaching and learning mathematics may require direct support and coaching from instructional leaders and peer coaches. The mathematics problem in figure 3.7 (page 78) is an example of concept-rich mathematics. It calls for far more than simply solving the problem. Computational skills are a given. Additionally, students are expected to make decisions about how to solve the problem—formulating—and show through drawings how they solved the problem—representing. In brief, students are now being asked to solve, show, and explain. The pie chart illustrates the idea of concept-rich problem solving. Rather than solving a problem and choosing a, b, c, or d as the correct answer, students are expected to think, using logic and reasoning, to find the solution and to be able to explain what they have done and why.

Conceptual understanding is key to students completing the task in figure 3.7. The real-world example of the pizza decision is conceptually rich for students because it requires them to compare and contrast two similar products, make a decision based on the facts present (start with the knowns), formulate the problem (figure out what I need to do), and represent the information graphically (draw what I know), as well as calculate consumer pricing advantages (use the division operation to calculate and other math tools to confirm—check forward and backward). Common Core mathematics highlights overarching concepts as the basis for long-lasting mathematical understandings that will serve students in solving real-world problems. That is not to say that computational and calculation skills are not necessary components of a comprehensive mathematics curriculum. The CCSS expect students to do the computations and calculations as somewhat automatic responses once they have mastered the functions. However, reasoning about mathematics is paramount. Developing this skill is going to take time, energy, and leadership support before it begins to permeate mathematics instruction in our schools.

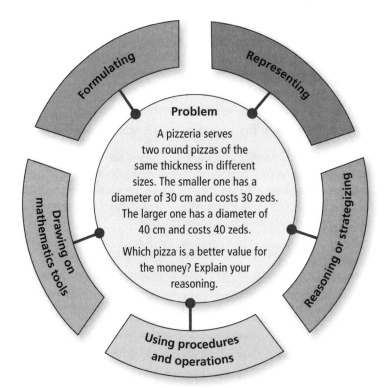

Figure 3.7: An example of a concept-rich mathematics problem.

Source: OECD, 2010a, p. 34.

Concept Approach to Mathematics

The mathematical concepts in the CCSS include similar big ideas across the grades (see for example, table 1.1, page 23) that are representative of the maturity of the students. These include typical mathematics sequences such as number sense, equations and expressions, geometry, measurement, and probability and statistics. Geometry is one domain that applies across K–8 in the CCSS for mathematics. Additionally, Geometry is one of the conceptual categories in the high school CCSS for mathematics. Table 3.3 (page 80) provides an overview of topics in the Geometry domain for kindergarten through grade 8.

Real-World Approach to Mathematics

Another hallmark of the Common Core mathematics is the expectation that teachers apply concepts and computational solutions not just to mathematics problems in a textbook but also within real-world contexts. Figure 3.8 (page 81) shows examples for the grade 5 domain Measurement and Data and for the grade 6 domain Geometry.

An example of using the Measurement and Data domain in the real world is one involving painting and carpeting a room in your home. The measurement data is in inches, while the paint data is in quarts and gallons and the carpet is in square yards. It takes conceptual understanding to convert all of this information in order to know how much of each of the materials to buy. Applying the concept of right triangles in the building and construction business is an example of a real-world use of the Geometry standard. Deep understanding of such concepts is necessary for architectural designers and engineers. *Real world* means students might apply these concepts in model building or simulated computer-aided design or manufacturing (CAD/CAM) program drawings of the real thing. One example of these CAD/CAM programs is designing a three-dimensional image or model of a working robotic device for later construction. These authentic projects are evidence of the relevant and real-world applications.

Moving to a concept-rich mathematics approach is not easy for teachers or students because of the traditional skill-and-drill approach to mathematics computation and simple plug-and-play calculations. This approach may require additional professional development opportunities to support teachers as they become more skillful in designing and implementing lessons from the concept-rich perspective.

Table 3.3: CCSS for Mathematics Geometry Domain Clusters, K–8

Kinder-garten	Grade 1	Grade 2	Grade 3	Grade 4	Grade 5	Grade 6	Grade 7	Grade 8
Identify and describe shapes. Analyze, compare, create, and compose shapes.	Reason with shapes and their attributes.	Reason with shapes and their attributes.	Reason with shapes and their attributes.	Draw and identify lines and angles, and classify shapes by properties of their lines and angles.	Graph points on the coordinate plane to solve real-world and mathematical problems. Classify two-dimensional figures into categories based on their properties.	Solve real-world and mathematical problems involving area, surface area, and volume.	Draw, construct, and describe geometrical figures and describe the relationships between them. Solve real-life and mathematical problems involving angle measure, area, surface area, and volume.	Understand congruence and similarity using physical models, transparencies, or geometry software. Understand and apply the Pythagorean theorem. Solve real-world and mathematical problems involving volume of cylinders, cones, and spheres.

Source: Adapted from NGA & CCSSO, 2010e, pp. 10, 14, 18, 22, 28, 34, 41, 47, and 53.

Domain: Measurement and Data (5.MD)

Cluster: Convert like measurement units within a given measurement system.

5.MD.A.1: Convert among different-sized standard measurement units within a given measurement system (for example, convert 5 cm to 0.05 m), and use these conversions in solving multistep, real-world problems.

Domain: Geometry (6.G)

Cluster: Solve real-world and mathematical problems involving area, surface area, and volume.

6.G.A.1: Find the area of right triangles, other triangles, special quadrilaterals, and polygons by composing into rectangles or decomposing into triangles and other shapes; apply these techniques in the context of solving real-world and mathematical problems.

Figure 3.8: Common Core mathematics applications in real-world contexts.

Inquiry Learning

The concept of real-world applications is central to the missions of the CCSS and the Partnership for 21st Century Skills (www.p21.org). Problem solving, creativity, and innovation manifest themselves in authentic projects and performances. Indeed, it was PISA's testing of real-world problems that provoked much of the concern about the failure of U.S. students to demonstrate these skills (OECD, 2009). It is through these complex problems and resulting projects and performances that students genuinely apply the knowledge and skills from the academic world of the classroom. This is how inert knowledge becomes applied knowledge. It is how students utilize the learning in practical and inventive ways.

Inquiry learning is a broad term that encompasses instructional activities that engage students in developing projects, performing, innovating, and solving problems. The critical attribute that distinguishes inquiry learning from traditional practices is the student-driven aspect. This feature empowers students to plan and to implement their ideas in hands-on projects that involve challenging problem solving throughout. While students are ultimately responsible for the project completion, teachers guide this work with miniskill lessons, coaching, feedback, deadlines, and due dates that propel the student work. The domain Research to Build and Present Knowledge in the Writing strand of the Common Core ELA defines expectations consistent with the principles of inquiry learning.

> ## WRITING ANCHOR STANDARDS IN DOMAIN RESEARCH TO BUILD AND PRESENT KNOWLEDGE
>
> **CCRA.W.7:** Conduct short as well as more sustained research projects based on focused questions, demonstrating understanding of the subject under investigation.
>
> **CCRA.W.8:** Gather relevant information from multiple print and digital sources, assess the credibility and accuracy of each source, and integrate the information while avoiding plagiarism.
>
> **CCRA.W.9:** Draw evidence from literary or informational texts to support analysis, reflection, and research.
>
> *Source: NGA & CCSSO, 2010b, p. 18.*

Inquiry learning can be independent or highly collaborative, depending on the purpose, the time allotted, and the type of task. When collaborations are integral to the inquiry design, they provide a level of student support that is needed as students learn to address the social skills of productive teamwork. The Speaking and Listening strand in the CCSS ELA provides direction for behaviors necessary for student success in inquiry-based activities.

The Three Cs of Inquiry Learning

Project-based learning is based on the foundational work of John Dewey (1938), which describes hands-on experiential learning. In his seminal book *Experience and Education*, Dewey (1938) presents the idea that the community is the classroom that allows for authentic and experiential learning using the resources at hand. Following that philosophy, the three Cs of inquiry learning identify three key elements that permeate the Common Core State Standards: content mastery, critical thinking, and collaboration.

1. **Content mastery** develops from standards-based projects that demonstrate evidence of deep learning.
2. **Critical thinking** develops from mindful problem solving and innovative applications.
3. **Collaboration** develops cooperative skills needed for leadership, teamwork, social interaction, and conflict resolution.

SPEAKING AND LISTENING ANCHOR STANDARDS

Domain: Comprehension and Collaboration

CCRA.SL.1: Prepare for and participate effectively in a range of conversations and collaborations with diverse partners, building on others' ideas and expressing their own clearly and persuasively.

CCRA.SL.2: Integrate and evaluate information presented in diverse media and formats, including visually, quantitatively, and orally.

CCRA.SL.3: Evaluate a speaker's point of view, reasoning, and use of evidence and rhetoric.

Domain: Presentation of Knowledge and Ideas

CCRA.SL.4: Present information, findings, and supporting evidence such that listeners can follow the line of reasoning and the organization, development, and style are appropriate to task, purpose, and audience.

CCRA.SL.5: Make strategic use of digital media and visual displays of data to express information and enhance understanding of presentations.

CCRA.SL.6: Adapt speech to a variety of contexts and communicative tasks, demonstrating command of formal English when indicated or appropriate.

Source: NGA & CCSSO, 2010b, p. 22.

Using end-of-unit projects is common in traditional schools. The emergence of inquiry learning in its various iterations gives a new emphasis to projects, performances, and products as the focus of learning throughout units of study rather than as add-ons. The distinction is that the inquiry—problem solving, investigation, exploration, and experimentation—becomes the method for learning, not merely the final statement. In place of learning *by* simply doing—what might be dubbed the *rub-off effect* of traditional projects—inquiry learning experiences include structured learning *from* doing tasks during the unit and reflecting on the *how* and *why* of the combined practical and academic work. Students do not work in isolation in inquiry learning activities. In these projects, teacher-stimulated reflections help students think about what and how they learned, so, as adroit problem solvers, they may transfer their new knowledge and skills to increasingly complex and difficult challenges in the curriculum. As with explicit teaching, close reading, and concept-rich mathematics instruction, school leaders must champion inquiry learning and the various forms it takes in the classroom. In fact, they may be instrumental in coaching for sound rubrics that assign appropriate values to the quality of student work in these projects. Remember, what is assessed is what is valued.

Inquiry-centered end-of-unit projects like dioramas, collages, mobiles, and flour-and-salt contour maps in the elementary grades or science projects, art shows, and gym demonstrations in the middle grades provide a beginning to performances and project-based learning within the inquiry learning family. However, more robust inquiry learning has several distinctions. The four features of robust inquiry learning are the following.

1. Units often start with an ill-defined problem or a driving question that may originate from the teacher or the students.

2. Students, working with partners or small groups, then refine the question or problem with research that clarifies the challenge or issue.

3. Students analyze the data, evaluate ideas, deepen their understanding, and make judgments.

4. Students decide how and what they are going to communicate about what they have learned, plan their product, and prepare a presentation of some kind.

Inquiry learning raises the bar on classroom instruction, because it is more student-centered, student-directed, and student-produced than the direct-design model that places the teacher front and center. In the inquiry learning model, the teacher may give instruction in skills and concepts needed to complete the inquiry, yet the teacher is a guide on the side most of the time. In this new role, the teacher facilitates and coaches, as well as instructs. It moves the learning to the realm of the practical, real world.

Authentic Questions

One of the most challenging tasks for teacher teams implementing inquiry learning is identifying relevant, authentic questions and problems that will connect student learning to issues and concerns that impact students' daily lives in and out of school. This becomes another teachable moment for staff, as leaders model and demonstrate the differences between academic questions that have right answers and essential questions that provoke thinking for multiple answers.

Relevant, authentic questions concern universal ideas that have reach and are generalizable to multiple situations. An authentic question asks the unanswerable because there are many interpretations. What is just? (moral dilemma) How do we determine beauty? (philosophical understanding) Do good fences make good neighbors? (values interpretation)

On the other hand, there are valid and worthwhile academic questions that lead students along the learning pathways. Yet, these questions must not be mistaken for the overarching authentic questions that rule our universe. Academic questions include complex but answerable questions. How high are mountain ranges? How does democracy work?

Effective questions that drive student inquiry are those that cannot be answered with the flood of facts from an Internet search. Situations that lack a clear-cut answer must promote real-world problem solving (OECD, 2010b). Teachers can prime students by starting with a grade-level Reading standard (literature or informational text) and encourage students to identify a key problem in the material they read. Such real-world issues as graffiti in the park, cell-phone use on public transportation or in the classroom, wounded veterans, preteen drinking, and animal rights prove to be popular choices.

The process begins when students define the relevant issue's parameters in a scenario, assume stakeholder roles that represent distinct points of view, and embark on the search for information. They refine the problem, research the facts, explore best- or worst-case scenarios, generate alternatives, and decide on possible, probable, and preferred solutions before preparing how they will communicate their findings. Throughout, teachers foster students' creative- and critical-thinking skills as they move back and forth in their investigation of the issue. In addition to having the students learn the content that is embedded in the solution search, teachers guide students' development as explorers, generators, analyzers, judges, and creative talents (OECD, 2010b).

Leaders supporting Common Core implementation are quick to applaud these efforts toward more authentic learning in the classroom. They understand the effort to make the learning not only rigorous but also genuinely relevant to young people. Effective leaders provide rich professional development experiences that translate readily into classroom action. OECD (2010b) states:

> Good teaching promotes self-regulated learning and metacognition and develops the cognitive processes that underpin problem solving. It prepares students to reason effectively in unfamiliar situations, and to fill gaps in their knowledge by observation, exploration, and interaction with unknown systems. (p. 9)

Primary-Grades Lesson

From Worms to Wall Street (George Lucas Educational Foundation, 2001), an Edutopia video, is a must-see for insight into what contributes to effective inquiry learning. The video shows kindergarten students from Newsome Park Elementary School in a full-scale project-based learning unit that is connected to multiple, cross-disciplinary standards. From a classroom-generated question about worms, the students eventually plan a business that sells stock. The question not only builds on an outside-the-classroom interest of these young students but prompts them to solve a significant ill-defined problem, generates both critical and creative thinking that allows for open-ended responses with multiple possible solutions, and encourages collaboration and communication with robust standards-aligned content. This is the kind of robust inquiry-learning experience that leaders can spotlight for discussion to encourage others to step out and try project learning. The reproducible "Assessing Inquiry-Based Learning" (page 93) is an example of a resource leaders can use to consider inquiry-based activities.

Middle-Grades Lesson

In an inquiry-based lesson for seventh graders on research skills, the teacher frames the research tasks around a history lesson on World War II. Enhancing the search aspect of the research skills, she uses the latest and greatest Internet-based technology to motivate these history-weary students.

Using Quick Response codes (QR codes) like the ones that appear on storefronts and magazine ads for immediate links to retail websites, the teacher generates research questions that she emails to the student teams. The teacher uses a QR code generator website (www.qrstuff.com) to produce codes that are linked to various resources that hold the answers to the questions.

QR CODES

QR codes: QR codes are signage in the form of a barcode that appear on storefronts and magazine ads. These codes can be accessed on any smartphone or tablet by downloading a QR code reader app that redirects the code to a website using the phone's web browser. The reader connects to a website for information.

QR code generator websites: QR code generator websites instantly create the codes. You simply find the link or text you want coded and place it in the message box on the site. A code is generated for you to download and sent by email or text.

Using questions that student teams must investigate as part of the project, the teacher prints and places color-coded QR codes around the classroom. Each QR code contains a website or immediate link to the question asked. This tool takes students to a wide variety of resources for the project.

The teacher organizes the class into teams of five students. Each team has five roles and responsibilities to execute the task, and each team is assigned a different color.

1. **Receiver:** Scans QR codes

2. **Researcher:** Finds source and information needed

3. **Recorder:** Gathers and assembles the information

4. **Restoration expert:** Helps direct the presentation format

5. **Reporter:** Reports findings

Each team begins its search at a different QR code question. With each team using a different QR code question, the teacher uses a jigsaw model to manage the groups. The groups end the inquiry-based lesson with a presentation using the Apple application Keynote (instead of PowerPoint), which focuses on which resources they used to find the answers about the war. The lesson result shows that students are focused on learning how to do worthy research as well as gaining information about history.

This lesson example shows the three Cs of inquiry learning in action (see page 82): (1) *content mastery* (framing a standards-based history lesson), (2) *critical thinking* (deciding on the best resources and answers to the questions), and (3) *collaboration* (assigning each team member a role and responsibility).

School leaders recognize the value of such lessons in implementing the CCSS. They understand the effort to make the learning not only rigorous but also more relevant with the focus on research skills and by utilizing contemporary technology tools.

Secondary-Grades Lesson

A tenth-grade geometry class is completing a unit on the Pythagorean theorem when the teacher challenges student teams to apply the theory to a model or structure. Students arrange themselves in teams and brainstorm all kinds of possibilities for putting the Pythagorean theorem to use. They research how to apply mathematical ideas, plot, plan, and develop blueprints of the structures. As part of the project, the students build models incorporating the right triangles as discussed in the theory. They make birdhouses, shelves, cupboards, and a doghouse. One team stumbles on the idea of building an actual handicap ramp for a neighbor who uses a walker and cannot get down her back steps.

Looking Back

Moving from the Common Core State Standards to instructional excellence that supports the rigor and relevance needed for all students to be college and career ready requires the leader's skilled eye and alert ear. Teachers signal what they want and need in order to do their jobs with expertise. At the same time, school leaders provide the vision and opportunity for innovation as they support teachers in making the transition to new practices the CCSS clearly articulate. The role of the leader and staff member is to define how to institute the CCSS with effectiveness and fidelity.

Making professional decisions (on-your-seat and on-your-feet decisions) to craft and implement the best practices of explicit instruction, close reading of text, concept-rich mathematics instruction, and inquiry learning, leaders and teachers turn the 21st century classroom into an exciting beehive of activity. With rich academic content and rigorous thinking processes, students have the needed tools to explore, investigate, invent, and innovate with relevant projects and performances. While there are other worthy instructional models, these are examples of the kind of learning that is required in 21st century classrooms.

Discussion Questions

The discussion questions are for collaborative, grade-level, or department teams or even just two colleagues working together or with a principal as part of a staff meeting to discuss this chapter as part of a book study or as a stand-alone chapter with good information and examples for rigorous and relevant learning. There is nothing as powerful as reflective conversation among professionals.

1. How is instructional excellence integral to the successful implementation of the Common Core State Standards? Provide specific examples.

2. Common Core can be a game changer for instructional delivery. Do you agree or disagree? Justify your thinking.

3. Rank the four instructional models featured in this chapter in the order that seems most appropriate for your staff to add to their teaching and learning repertoires. Explain your reasoning.

    _____ Explicit instruction of thinking skills

    _____ Close reading of text

    _____ Concept-rich mathematics instruction

    _____ Inquiry learning

4. How skillful are your teachers with authentic implementation of the Common Core? Use the following rating scale to assess their skill. Explain your answer with specific examples. Is a pattern evident in your ratings? If so, what does that pattern suggest for future professional development activities?

    a. Well on the way

    b. Ready, willing, and able

    c. Able but not that willing

    d. Willing, yet needing lots of support

    e. It depends!

Takeaways

In a final look back, consider the following takeaways for this chapter. These are just some of the learnings that will benefit you as you support, observe, and evaluate great instruction.

- Explicit instruction model: Talk-Through, Walk-Through, and Drive-Through

- Close reading of text analysis model: RSVPE

- Concept-rich mathematics that focus on reasoning and logic and common sense

- Inquiry learning to ignite student ownership of the learning

- Digital tools to integrate into the 21st century student-centered classrooms (QR codes)

Phase I: The Talk-Through—
Explicit Teaching Lesson

Target thinking skill	
Motivational mindset: A hook to engage students	
Description: The elements of the target thinking skill	
Order of operations: How-to steps for students	
Instructional strategy: Activity to address the target thinking skill	
Assessment: Evaluation of the product or performance	
Metacognitive reflection: Class analysis of the learning for future application	

Phase II: The Walk-Through—
Classroom Application Lesson

Target thinking skill	
Motivational mindset	
Standards-based lesson with application of targeted thinking skill	
Closure with reflection activity	

Phase III: The Drive-Through—
Common Core Performance Task Lesson

Standard	
Target thinking skill	
Motivational mindset	
Standards-based lesson with application of targeted thinking skill	
Independent performance task	
Closure with reflection activity that ensures student learning	

Assessing Inquiry-Based Learning

To what degree is the question authentic and essential?

1. Does the question fit with an outside-of-school living or working world question?

   ☐ Not Yet   ☐ Somewhat   ☐ Moderately   ☐ Strong

2. Does the question generate students' interest?

   ☐ Not Yet   ☐ Somewhat   ☐ Moderately   ☐ Strong

3. Does the question create a significant real-world, ill-defined problem?

   ☐ Not Yet   ☐ Somewhat   ☐ Moderately   ☐ Strong

4. Does the question generate critical- and creative-thinking proficiencies for problem solving?

   ☐ Not Yet   ☐ Somewhat   ☐ Moderately   ☐ Strong

5. Does the question allow for open-ended responses with multiple possible solutions?

   ☐ Not Yet   ☐ Somewhat   ☐ Moderately   ☐ Strong

6. Is the question manageable in given time constraints?

   ☐ Not Yet   ☐ Somewhat   ☐ Moderately   ☐ Strong

7. Does the question encourage rich application of 21st century skills standards?

   ☐ Not Yet   ☐ Somewhat   ☐ Moderately   ☐ Strong

8. Does the question align with standards from two or more disciplines?

   ☐ Not Yet   ☐ Somewhat   ☐ Moderately   ☐ Strong

Source: Adapted from Bellanca, 2012.

CHAPTER 4

The Shift in Coaching and Feedback

Leading With Guiding Principles

If your actions inspire others to dream more, learn more, do more and become more, you are a leader.

—John Quincy Adams

Mrs. Waddle, Ms. Hopper, Mrs. Flier, and Ms. High Stepper all teach in the same K–12 school. As the principal, Mr. Coacher observes in various classrooms, and his time with each teacher following the classroom visit becomes a teachable moment. He has learned how to give constructive feedback framed by five guiding principles, to move each teacher along, regardless of where she is currently in her professional learning journey. If the teachers are waddling, he helps them move forward; if they are hopping, he coaches them into a smoother stride; if they are flying, he gives them direction for flights extraordinaire; and if they are high-stepping, he inspires them with a sense of mission. His collegial spirit is the hallmark of his success, as he always ends each visit with a welcoming, "Invite me back."

Instructional leaders have the daunting task of walking in and out of many classrooms and making decisions about teaching and learning on a daily basis. The real purpose for observing classrooms is to improve student achievement. This can only be accomplished through improved teaching and learning. As schools begin to move from state standards to the CCSS, the time that leaders spend understanding what implementation looks like is crucial to a school's success. After schools have aligned and assessed the current curriculum, principals must support the Common Core State Standards using the R&I approach (see page 30) through observations and constructive feedback.

Five Effective Leadership Principles

We define five leadership principles to frame the activities that principals and other school leaders undertake as they work with teachers to implement the CCSS ELA/literacy and mathematics. These principles provide support for leaders as they observe classroom instruction, guide alignment of lessons to the CCSS, facilitate coaching conversations, extend invitations to revisit the classroom, and converse about data results.

Principle One: Walk In, Talk It Out

Effective principals look for rich content, rigorous performance, and relevant thinking as they observe classroom instruction. To ensure that students have opportunities to become productive problem solvers, sound decision makers, and creative innovators, educational leaders must balance rich content with relevant thinking skills as they implement the CCSS. To do this effectively, classroom instruction using the CCSS must reflect an emphasis on the explicit teaching of complex thinking skills within the content areas. The two go hand in hand. Otherwise, we will simply make the same mistakes we have made with the first move to a standards-based curriculum. We will water down the intent with mundane, fact-and-recall assessments that will then drive the instructional landscape.

The only way to know if complex thinking is occurring is through listening to discussions, being in the classroom, and asking students questions during instructional time. Informal observations are the first steps to the high-level planning necessary for moving toward using the Common Core State Standards. Valerie von Frank (2013) suggests that acute observers notice what's important in teaching practice, know what to look for in curriculum units, take objective notes that describe student learning, and avoid using technology during the classroom visits.

Principle Two: Align Lessons to the CCSS

"How are the CCSS different from what we're already doing?" is the paramount question in all educators' minds as they learn about the standards. As the instructional leader in the building, the principal must sit in the driver's seat and lead the change. First and foremost to facilitate change, the principal needs to become familiar with the CCSS. The principal is responsible for leading professional conversations with teachers to move the school forward while staying focused on the core premises of the CCSS: fewer standards, increased rigor and relevance, and clear expectations.

The CCSS affirm what students should be able to do by the end of the year. Principals must know how to unpack the standards as they relate to content unit development. They must delve into performance assessments and figure out how learning looks as students progress from the factual to the conceptual to the application or extension phase of learning. As NGA and CCSSO (2010b) state, "While the Standards make references to some particular forms of content, including mythology, foundational U.S. documents, and Shakespeare, they do not—indeed cannot—enumerate all or even most of the content that students should learn" (p. 6). Therefore, leaders must remember the CCSS are not a curriculum, and the responsibility for course development will be at the local level.

To advance change in instructional practice, school leaders and teachers engage in a variety of tasks. They develop units around content topics. They use backward mapping to ensure continuity in concept development. They familiarize themselves with text features that contribute to complexity in both literature and informational texts. This awareness enables them to select texts that are grade and age appropriate as well as representative of both fiction and nonfiction. Additionally, the teachers choose texts that reflect the CCSS staircase effect of increasing text complexity. They structure lessons so that students receive some knowledge and experiences to build on as they encounter new material. This planning enables students to participate actively in classroom discussions or group work. Teachers use explicit teaching to support students as they learn new skills such as argumentation or persuasive writing. Such skill learning is less stressful for students when presented in the context of a unit or theme. Administrators who understand what is involved in aligning lessons with the CCSS are prepared for coaching opportunities that specifically explain how the CCSS are different from teaching and learning using current practices.

Principle Three: Facilitate Coaching Conversations

After observing a lesson, the principal needs to have a conversation with the teacher that allows the teacher an opportunity to reflect about the work the principal observed during his or her visit. According to Randi Weingarten (2011), president of the American Federation of Teachers:

> As important as evaluation is to assessing teacher performance, what passes for teacher evaluation in many districts frankly isn't up to this important task. Way too often, teacher evaluations are superficial. They're subjective. They miss a prime opportunity to improve teacher practice and, thereby, increase student learning. And that's what it's all about, isn't it?

The conversation should focus on teacher practice and student outcomes. The following questions are optimal for leading the change because they foster reflection about practice and help sustain a collegial conversation.

- How is the task aligned to the CCSS?
- How is the lesson a part of a unit?
- What did you want students to be able to do at the end of the lesson?

- Are you creating, developing, or enriching curious students by focusing on the process and not the answer?

- Does the task require students to think and use information from the text?

- How do students know when they're successful? Can all learners succeed?

- Are the texts at the appropriate level of complexity for the grade?

Principle Four: Invite Me Back

Instructional leaders invest lots of time collecting student-work samples as evidence of teaching and learning. The purpose of this collection is to ensure rigor in instruction and verification of student achievement. However, the work becomes cumbersome for leaders if indeed this is the method they are using for all teachers of all grades. During much of the school day, principals can find themselves reading through mounds of paperwork as opposed to spending time in the classroom. The *invite me back* principle is built on the premise that the principal and teacher have had some discussion about instruction and changes that the teacher can implement immediately. After such a discussion in which the teacher and principal exchange ideas for making the lesson more rigorous, the principal should extend the invitation: "Invite me back to your classroom to watch the changes unfold." The invitation opens the door for future conversations. The teacher leaves with a plan, and the principal has a date for another visit. All leaders know that what's expected must be inspected. They also know that good conversations inspire people. Therefore, the next visit should be centered on a mutually agreed-on discussion point from the conversation.

Principle Five: Have Data-Informed Peer Conversations

Creating a culture that fosters and enhances collaboration is essential in a time of change. When teachers have opportunities to share their *aha* moments and their hurdles as they create learning experiences for students that focus on analyzing, evaluating, and problem solving, collaboration is organic. Often, teachers work together cooperatively around a project or a compliance task set forth by administration. Organic collaboration is natural and purposeful when the conversation is around student data. The job of the leader is to provide the time for grade-level or departmental collaborative teams to meet and focus the conversation on content-specific material. By looking at real data, the team conversations can focus on *what* students are learning. Creating a mobile data wall or board that incorporates both summative and formative data that focus on student needs is a quick win for school leaders. Data walls are useful if they are mobile or in a location where meetings are held for ease of referencing students and citing as sources for information. Data walls are valuable if they track assessments that guide instruction. They are also beneficial if progress monitoring of students can be tracked over time by examining instructional strategies. Finally, data walls are useful if conclusions can be drawn about instruction. For example, see figure 4.1 (page 100).

The first table represents the way a third grade language arts teacher tracks students using data. She looks at an instructional strategy that is part of CCSS RI.3.1 and RL.3.1; answering text-dependent questions. Every month students are assessed and placed on the data wall. Developing Students are working below the 70th percentile; Meeting Students are working between the 70-89th percentile; and Exceeding Students have mastered the strategy/skill and are meeting the 90th percentile each month. This data chart creates opportunity for discussion around: are my students learning and how do I know?

The second table represents an eighth grade math teacher's data wall that was developed by performance assessment based on CCSS 8.F.B.5. Developing Students are working below the 70th percentile; Meeting Students are working between the 70-89th percentile; and Exceeding Students have mastered the strategy/skill and are meeting the 90th percentile each month. After reviewing the performance assessments, the teacher records concerns and next steps for both Developing Students and Meeting Students. This data chart creates opportunity for discussion around next steps: how will I provide intervention, enrichment, and small-group instruction for my students?

Once teachers identify struggling learners in the classroom, the conversations, observations, and data walls should all focus on data driving the student learning. Essentially, during the informal observation, the principal should walk into the observation with the names of the struggling learners. This way, he or she focuses careful attention on observing the struggling learners to see if teacher questioning is making a difference. The goal is to have teachers planning collectively to develop new strategies based on analysis. Data-informed peer conversations focus on student learning and should be continuous. These conversations focus on analyzing the units teachers planned, performance tasks they established, and current lessons students are working on in the classroom, not on looking at numbers and reporting out. Data analysis as a collaborative practice creates an atmosphere of inquiry and collective responsibility that results in a shared understanding of the need to change teaching and learning practices to increase student achievement (Price & Koretz, 2005).

The Principles in Practice

To make the implementation of the CCSS come alive, we present a quartet of fictionalized accounts of our personal experiences with school leaders and teachers. These vignettes illustrate the five guiding principles for effective school leadership. The scenarios feature a principal's (Mr. Coacher) observations of a fifth-grade

Instructional strategy: Text-dependent questions		
Developing Students **September 2, 2013**	**Meeting Students** **September 2, 2013**	**Exceeding Students** **September 2, 2013**
MJ Brown SP Scott CB Charles	MD Room WN Kot	HA Stems
Developing Students October 2, 2013	**Meeting Students** October 2, 2013	**Exceeding Students** October 2, 2013
CB Charles	MJ Brown SP Scott MD Room WN Kot	HA Stems
Developing Students November 2, 2013	**Meeting Students** November 2, 2013	**Exceeding Students** November 2, 2013
CB Charles	WN Kot	HA Stems MJ Brown SP Scott MD Room

Performance task: Given two situations, students can determine the relationship using functions and explain discoveries.		
Developing Students	**Meeting Students**	**Exceeding Students**
MJ Brown	SP Scott MD Room WN Kot	CB Charles HA Stems
Concerns Students are having difficulty deciding which operation to use to solve word problems with multiple steps. **What's Next?** Small-group instruction with solving problems relating to functions.	**Concerns** Students need assistance with citing evidence for discoveries. **What's Next?** Collaborative group discussions that focus on real-world problems that require explanation and consensus during RTI (response to intervention) period.	**The Push** Students will benefit from making determinations based on discoveries. **What's Next?** Independent problem solving practice for students who are ready to work on their own.

Figure 4.1: Sample data walls.

teacher's reading lesson in which students are making predictions; a second-grade teacher's reading lesson in which students are working with questions in a guided reading activity; an eighth-grade teacher's mathematics lesson; and a ninth-grade teacher's biology lesson. The vignettes describe observations for each of the five guiding principles for leadership and include references to appropriate Common Core ELA/literacy and mathematics standards. As a reminder to himself, Mr. Coacher notes that he needs to read through the observation notes from previous visits and during the observation make mental notes of the teacher's moves that could be enhanced through coaching conversations.

Vignette One: Mrs. Waddle's Fifth-Grade Reading Lesson

Mrs. Waddle's traditional classroom always produced good results using strategies around reading text and answering questions. Mrs. Waddle used the basal readers daily and relied heavily on the teaching notes in the teacher's edition when questioning her students throughout the unit. Moving to the Common Core State Standards, Mrs. Waddle began to create purposeful lessons around a theme that required students to think.

Principle One: Walk In, Talk It Out

During this observation in Mrs. Waddle's classroom, Mr. Coacher watches intently to gain a sense of how she conducts the lesson and how the students respond. This visit provides the context for conversations he and Mrs. Waddle will have about her teaching and the students' learning.

Observation Focus: Mrs. Waddle is teaching a fifth-grade reading lesson on prediction.

Observation Summary: Twenty-five fifth graders focus on the teacher, listening eagerly with their theme books open and tape on their desks. The teacher reads a paragraph from a short story, "The Dinner Party" by Mona Gardner (1941) from the book *Sudden Twists*, on the SMART Board while the students follow along. The learning target is on the chalkboard: "Students will be able to make predictions." After the teacher finishes reading the paragraph, she distributes a copy of the first paragraph to each student and asks, "What do you think will happen next?" Students tape the paragraph to their theme books and write what they think will happen next. There's a buzz of activity in the room, and the teacher begins sampling the students for answers. The predictions are interesting and focus on text-to-world connections. Students' guesses revolve around their homes, their family lives, and stories they have heard or seen on television. The lesson continues with much excitement. The teacher sustains her students' enthusiasm and completes the story that has a sudden twist that surprises the students.

Principle Two: Align Lessons to the CCSS

Mr. Coacher's familiarity with the CCSS enables him to identify the Common Core standards Mrs. Waddle addresses in her lesson.

Observation Focus: Students will be able to verify their predictions.

Observation Summary: The lesson focused on a Reading Standard for Literature in the domain Key Ideas and Details at the fifth-grade level. The anchor standard and grade-level standard follow.

> **CCRA.R.1:** Read closely to determine what the text says explicitly and to make logical inferences from it; cite specific textual evidence when writing or speaking to support conclusions drawn from the text. (NGA & CCSSO, 2010a, p. 10)

> **RL.5.1:** Quote accurately from the text when explaining what the text says explicitly and when drawing inferences from the text. (NGA & CCSSO, 2010a, p. 12)

Principle Three: Facilitate Coaching Conversations

Mr. Coacher identifies seven questions to organize the coaching conversations he and Mrs. Waddle will have about her instruction. The questions focus on CCSS alignment, lesson development, student engagement, and text complexity.

Observation Focus 1: How is the task aligned to the CCSS?

Observation Summary 1: The skill of predicting is *not* a fifth-grade standard. Since there are fewer standards with increased rigor, it is necessary to understand the difference between predicting and inferring. When students are asked to predict, they are simply being asked to do what is called *advance inferring* based on the text, the author, and their background knowledge. Inferring involves reading all of the evidence and making the best guess. When inferring, students use all clues to draw conclusions about what is being read. Proficient readers make predictions effortlessly and without much contemplation, and then verify or disprove them based on continued reading. The CCSS call for the conversation to be around the text. The standards are written so students use writing comprehension that focuses on drawing conclusions based on facts presented in the reading or closed reading strategy.

Observation Focus 2: How is the lesson a part of a unit?

Observation Summary 2: The teacher is working on a narrative writing unit. Every day she selects a different story to read aloud after lunch to point out how good writers utilize every moment of a story to give additional clues about the setting, plot, and characters.

Observation Focus 3: What did you want students to be able to do at the end of the lesson?

Observation Summary 3: The teacher wants the students to be able to use clues from the text to draw conclusions in the stories to see how to improve their writing. This is a very good goal, as it takes students from what the teacher wants them to understand, to showing what the students should know, and finally to what the teacher wants them to do. The teacher is already cross-referencing the CCSS because the lesson also has a writing goal.

Observation Focus 4: Are you creating, developing, or enriching curious students by focusing on the process and not the answer?

Observation Summary 4: The students are begging for more of the story, so they are definitely curious about what will happen next. Students are actively engaged and following along. They are also excited to share their predictions.

Observation Focus 5: Does the task require students to think and use information from the text?

Observation Summary 5: Students are able to make predictions but do not use information from the text explicitly.

The task could have had students describe the meaning behind their predictions using information from the text.

The task does require students to think and use information from the text. The teacher often skips over these important tasks. Through the excitement of the story and the sharing, the teacher misses critical teaching moments.

The students are often heard speaking and sharing predictions about their families at home and telling stories that do not utilize text connections. When the lesson has the direction of using inferences as opposed to making predictions, it changes the focus the teacher provides the students. The teacher could then begin the lesson with, "Today we are going to use clues from the text to make inferences about what will happen next in the story. These clues are what good writers use to make the reader want to read more."

Observation Focus 6: How do students know when they're successful? Can all learners succeed?

Observation Summary 6: Students feel successful because they are predicting and writing something down in their notebooks. Students are engaged in conversations about their predictions.

There were no expectations shared with students before the lesson except the learning target to make predictions. No rubrics are available, so the students have no idea about the level of their performance.

Observation Focus 7: Are the texts at the appropriate level of complexity for the grade?

Observation Summary 7: The text complexity is grade-level appropriate. These stories are typically designed for students in grades 6–8 to read.

Principle Four: Invite Me Back

As a result of their conversations, Mrs. Waddle and Mr. Coacher have agreed-on topics for his observations in his next visit to her classroom.

Observation Focus: The next visit will focus on these aspects of instruction.

- Does the task require students to think and use information from the text?
- How do students know when they're successful?
- Can all learners succeed?

Observation Summary: During the second observation, the teacher specifically asks questions to get students to draw conclusions and make sure students make predictions related to the text. She uses prompts like the following.

1. "What do you think will happen next based on the information presented?"
2. "Make sure you use examples from the story."
3. "When you share your prediction at your table, your partner must ask you why you think that will happen next."

The teacher decides to develop a performance task grading tool (table 4.1) that clearly defines behaviors of developing, meeting, and exceeding criteria.

Table 4.1: Mrs. Waddle's Performance Task Grading Tool

Criterion	Developing	Meeting	Exceeding
Students describe the meaning behind their predictions using information from the text.	Students make predictions after every section read.	Students make inferences about what will happen next in the story based on simple information from the text.	Students make inferences about what will happen next in the story based on more complex information (with explanation) from the text.

Principle Five: Have Data-Informed Peer Conversations

Mr. Coacher and Mrs. Waddle identify resources she can share with her team at its next meeting.

Observation Focus: What will the teacher bring to discuss at the grade-level team meeting?

- Evidence of improvement from the struggling learners (student-work samples)
- Reflection from the informal observations of student performance
- Additional interim assessments that target the same skills

Observation Summary: The teacher summarizes the lesson and discusses the importance of rigor with the CCSS. The takeaway for everyone is reading and writing grounded in evidence from the text.

The teacher brings work samples from both lessons and highlights three important additions to the lesson.

1. The teacher creates a graphic organizer to accompany the lesson to guide students through the thinking process.
2. The teacher shares the performance task grading tool that accompanied the second set of graded papers.
3. The teacher pairs students with peers who will keep them on task, and so they have a direct partner for sharing predictions.

Vignette Two: Ms. Hopper's Second-Grade Reading Lesson

Ms. Hopper's second graders love to read. Her students tell stories around whatever they are reading. To implement the Common Core State Standards, she created opportunities for her students to practice reading during her guided reading time and then answer questions with information explicitly stated in the text as opposed to answering questions with narrative stories from experiences in their lives.

Principle One: Walk In, Talk It Out

During this informal observation in Ms. Hopper's classroom, Mr. Coacher wants to ensure text complexity is executed when students read aloud during the guided reading period and ensure students can answer questions independently. This visit provides a springboard for conversations during grade-level team meetings about selecting text that requires rigor.

Observation Focus: Ms. Hopper is listening to groups of students read complex text and observing them as they implement the question-answer relationship (QAR) strategy.

Observation Summary: Five students from a second-grade class are in a guided-reading group. The students are reading a chapter, "The Garden," from the book *Frog and Toad Together* (Lobel, 1972). The students are reading with fluency. When the students complete reading, the teacher says she is going to review the questions they will answer independently at their desks. She tells the students there are two types of questions today: (1) *right there* questions, for which the answer is right there in the book, and (2) *in your head* questions, for which they have to think about the answer on their own and find the answer in their heads. The teacher gives examples of both types of questions.

She asks, "What did Toad say to his seeds to get them to grow?" The students respond that the answer to the question is found in the book.

She asks, "Have you ever planted seeds before?" The students respond that the answer to the question is in their heads. The teacher asks students to explain how they knew that the question was not based on information from the story, but information they already knew.

She asks, "What advice does Frog give Toad about growing seeds?" The students say they can find the answer in the book.

The teacher says, "Think about our science unit and the chapter we just read in *Frog and Toad Together*. What makes seeds grow best?" The students answer they have to use their heads to answer the question with information from both the story and material they learned in science.

Principle Two: Align Lessons to the CCSS

Mr. Coacher listens to second-grade students read with ease and fluency. He refers Ms. Hopper to appendix B of the Common Core ELA/literacy standards (NGA & CCSSO, 2010d) for text-appropriate examples for second grade.

Observation Focus: Students will be able to answer text-dependent questions and non-text-dependent questions.

Observation Summary: The lesson focused on a Reading Standard for Literature in the domain Range of Reading and Text Complexity. The anchor standard and grade-level standard follow.

> **CCRA.R.10:** Read and comprehend complex literary and informational texts independently and proficiently. (NGA & CCSSO, 2010a, p. 10)

RL.2.10: By the end of the year, read and comprehend literature, including stories and poetry, in the grades 2–3 text complexity band proficiently, with scaffolding as needed at the high end of the range. (NGA & CCSSO, 2010a, p. 11)

Principle Three: Facilitate Coaching Conversations

Mr. Coacher identifies seven questions to organize the coaching conversations. The questions focus on CCSS alignment, lesson development, student engagement, and text complexity.

Observation Focus 1: How is the task aligned to the CCSS?

Observation Summary 1: The students are reading independently and with a group, and they are going back to their seats to answer questions for understanding.

Observation Focus 2: How is the lesson a part of a unit?

Observation Summary 2: The unit is an author study of Arnold Lobel's *Frog and Toad* series.

Observation Focus 3: What did you want students to be able to do at the end of the lesson?

Observation Summary 3: Students should be able to read with fluency and answer questions explicitly referring to the book to form the basis for their answers.

Observation Focus 4: Are you creating, developing, or enriching curious students by focusing on the process and not the answer?

Observation Summary 4: Students read challenging text proficiently. Students also have to decide on the type of question before answering to create a thinking process for comprehension. The students are on task and answering the questions with relative ease.

Observation Focus 5: Does the task require students to think and use information from the text?

Observation Summary 5: Yes, the students are required to use the text to answer most of the questions presented. The lesson even presents opportunities for students to use information from their science lesson.

Observation Focus 6: How do students know when they're successful? Can all learners succeed?

Observation Summary 6: The teacher clearly reviewed directions, but she could have discussed the expected performance in further detail. All students could be successful! The lesson is presented in a small, differentiated group format lending itself easily to success for all with sufficient scaffolding.

Observation Focus 7: Are the texts at the appropriate level of complexity for the grade?

Observation Summary 7: According to appendix B of the Common Core State Standards (NGA & CCSSO, 2010d), the *Frog and Toad* books are exemplars for first grade. The text complexity was not grade-level appropriate. In the groundbreaking report "Reading Between the Lines," ACT (2006) finds, "Performance on complex texts is the clearest differentiator in reading between students who are more likely to be ready for college and those who are less likely to be ready" (p. 6).

Lily Fillmore (2010) writes, "Academic language can only be learned from texts—by noticing how it works in reading texts, engaging with, thinking about, discussing their content with others, and by writing" (p. 17).

Principle Four: Invite Me Back

Mr. Coacher and Ms. Hopper discuss factors the CC ELA/literacy define for grade-appropriate text. As a result of this discussion and others related to Mr. Coacher's observations during the reading lesson, they agree on ideas for text selection during unit planning.

Observation Focus: Are the texts at the appropriate level of complexity for the grade?

Observation Summary: Ms. Hopper initially selected the *Frog and Toad* series because she was doing an author study on Arnold Lobel. While meeting with Mr. Coacher, she looks through the exemplars in appendix B of the CCSS (NGA & CCSSO, 2010d) to get some ideas of the kind of literature that is considered grade appropriate. She selects a book from the list and goes through the task of comparing some of the differences between the text complexity of *Frog and Toad Together* and *Tops and Bottoms* by Janet Stevens (1995). She reflects on the language and the depth of the theme in *Tops and Bottoms* and develops a new unit plan and a new QAR lesson. Since students are in their differentiated reading groups, the teacher allows more time for struggling students to read the selections and complete the activities. During the lesson, Ms. Hopper talks with the students about the QAR strategy and how it helps them to understand the story.

Principle Five: Have Data-Informed Peer Conversations

Mr. Coacher and Ms. Hopper decide that at the next team meeting she can share her experiences about using Common Core ELA/literacy text exemplars during guided reading lessons.

Observation Focus: What will the teacher bring to discuss at the grade-level team meeting?

- Exemplars from the CCSS
- Evidence of differences in assignments (student-work samples)
- Reflection from the informal observations of student performance

Observation Summary: The teacher summarizes the lesson and discusses the importance of text complexity in the CCSS with her colleagues.

The teacher shares copies of both text and work samples struggling students completed in both lessons. The teachers evaluate the texts' quality by looking at the literary elements: setting, character, plot, theme, and style.

The teacher shares the performance task grading tool that accompanies the second set of graded papers. The teachers discuss how all lessons do not require rubrics but should have an intended outcome. The students review their papers as a class because the class needs regular practice with complex text and comprehension strategies.

Vignette Three: Mrs. Flier's Eighth-Grade Mathematics Lesson

Mrs. Flier's eighth-grade mathematics students are very good at taking notes and following steps to complete mathematical problems. As part of her implementation strategy for the CCSS, she incorporates reasons for the importance of learning mathematics. She creates performance assessments that require students to complete computations for problems, which resemble real-world applications.

Principle One: Walk In, Talk It Out

During this informal observation in Mrs. Flier's classroom, Mr. Coacher wants to see students making connections to real-life situations during an assessment. The visit provides the context for conversations he and Mrs. Flier will have about relevance in mathematics.

Observation Focus: Mrs. Flier is teaching an eighth-grade lesson on plotting patterns and determining the best buy.

Observation Summary: The teacher reviews objectives of the lesson with students. She says, "At the end of this lesson, you will be able to determine the better value of two cell-phone plans by plotting patterns and comparing linear graphs." All thirty-two eighth-grade girls have blank stares on their faces. The teacher distributes the problem of the day, and the class reads the first set of directions together.

- Plan A (standard): $30 for the first 500 minutes plus $0.60 per minute for every minute over
- Plan B (pay as you go): $0.25 a minute with no monthly fee

The energy in the class increases as the students begin predicting which cell-phone plan they would select before they get started on parts *a* and *b* of the problem.

a. Using a graph, plot total cost of each plan as a function of minutes called. The *x*-axis should be from 0 to 1,200 minutes.

b. On a separate sheet, write a paragraph comparing the two plans. In particular, address the consideration that would be helpful for someone making a decision about which plan to use.

The students immediately get to work creating their graphs and plotting their points. Many of the graphs look very different as students fill in their *x*-axis and *y*-axis.

Principle Two: Align Lessons to the CCSS

Mr. Coacher's understanding of the CCSS mathematics enables him to recognize the standards Mrs. Flier addresses in her lesson.

Observation Focus 1: Students will be able to plot patterns and compare linear graphs. Students will determine the better value.

Observation Summary 1: The lesson focused on a mathematics standard in the domains Expressions and Equations and Functions.

> **8.EE.5:** Graph proportional relationships, interpreting the unit rate as the slope of the graph. Compare two different proportional relationships represented in different ways. For example, compare a distance-time graph to a distance-time equation to determine which of two moving objects has greater speed. (NGA & CCSSO, 2010e, p. 54)

> **8.F.1:** Understand that a function is a rule that assigns to each input exactly one output. The graph of a function is the set of ordered pairs consisting of an input and the corresponding output. (NGA & CCSSO, 2010e, p. 55)

Principle Three: Facilitate Coaching Conversations

Mr. Coacher identifies seven questions to organize the coaching conversations. The questions focus on CCSS alignment, lesson development, student engagement, and text complexity.

Observation Focus 1: How is the task aligned to the CCSS?

Observation Summary 1: The tasks are well aligned because the assignment directly focuses on rigor, application, and assessment of an understanding of the problem through a written explanation.

Observation Focus 2: How is the lesson a part of a unit?

Observation Summary 2: The mathematics unit is on functions. Students should be able to define, evaluate, and compare functions. Students should also be able to use functions to model relationships between quantities.

Observation Focus 3: What did you want students to be able to do at the end of the lesson?

Observation Summary 3: The teacher identifies tasks at the beginning of the lesson. She says, "At the end of this lesson, you will be able to determine the better value of two cell-phone plans by plotting patterns and comparing linear graphs."

However, the teacher misses the opportunity to tell the students about writing for comprehension. She does not address the writing activity in the opening statement that clearly focuses on who should choose which plan. This is another lesson that spans across standards. Students need to see the coherence of the standards in every discipline. Since the students also have to compare the two plans and make some decisions about who should buy which plan, this is a missed performance task that the teacher didn't verbalize.

Observation Focus 4: Are you creating, developing, or enriching curious students by focusing on the process and not the answer?

Observation Summary 4: Students use the Mathematical Practices that spiral throughout all grade levels. Students use their mathematical knowledge and strategic skills with precision to solve the problem. Then they construct a viable argument about each plan.

Observation Focus 5: Does the task require students to think and use information from the text?

Observation Summary 5: Students use information for the problem of the day worksheet. Students have to think to get through the writing portion of the activity.

Observation Focus 6: How do students know when they're successful? Can all learners succeed?

Observation Summary 6: There are multiple steps for students to complete in this problem. The teacher has not developed a grading plan that could be shared with students.

Observation Focus 7: Are the texts at the appropriate level of complexity for the grade?

Observation Summary 7: Yes. The CCSS specifically state that grade 8 instructional time should focus on three critical areas.

1. Formulating and reasoning about expressions and equations, including modeling an association in bivariate data with a linear equation, and solving linear equations and systems of linear equations

2. Grasping the concept of a function and using functions to describe quantitative relationships

3. Analyzing two- and three-dimensional space and figures using distance, angle, similarity, and congruence, and understanding and applying the Pythagorean theorem (NGA & CCSSO, 2010e, p. 52)

Principle Four: Invite Me Back

As a result of their discussion about Mr. Coacher's Observation Summary 6 for principle three, he and Mrs. Flier agree that the performance assessment should include both computation and application tasks. Mr. Coacher reminds Mrs. Flier that a rubric to assess the performance task was missing from the lesson.

Observation Focus: How do students know when they're successful? Can all learners succeed?

Observation Summary: The teacher decides to develop a performance task grading tool (table 4.2) and use the work the students have already done to make changes to their work.

Students use a different colored writing utensil to show corrections to their work. The teacher passes out colored pencils to make sure everyone has an opportunity to do the assignment as requested.

The students use the rubric to recheck their work, and then they engage in peer review. The discussion is rich and allows all learners a chance to examine their work and improve what they have done.

Table 4.2: Mrs. Flier's Performance Task Grading Tool

Criterion	Developing	Meeting	Exceeding
Given two situations, students can determine the relationship using functions.	Students can solve problems relating to functions.	Students can determine the proportional relationship between two functions numerically and by graphing. Students will write about the discoveries.	Students can determine the proportional relationship between two functions numerically and by graphing. Students will write about the discoveries and give additional instances using real-life examples.

Principle Five: Have Data-Informed Peer Conversations

Mr. Coacher and Mrs. Flier pinpoint best practices with performance assessments that she can share with her team at its next meeting.

Observation Focus: What will the teacher bring to discuss at the grade-level team meeting?

- Evidence of improvement from using the performance task grading tool (student-work samples)
- Reflection from the informal observations of student performance

Observation Summary: The teacher summarizes the lesson and discusses the importance of coherence (thinking across grades with links to major topics) with the CCSS.

The teacher is able to look at what the students need to *understand*, *know*, and *do* to complete the assignment.

- **Understand:** The teacher shows struggling and top-performing students' work samples from the lesson, highlighting concepts students know.
- **Know:** The teacher shares the performance task grading tool with students, so they know what they were required to do.
- **Do:** Finally, the teacher highlights the application of mathematics that students compose to show their deep understanding of concepts and the difference between the state standards and the CCSS.

Vignette Four: Ms. High Stepper's Ninth-Grade Biology Lesson

Ms. High Stepper's departmentalized biology class integrates literacy strategies and encourages independence within a collaborative environment. She wants to create *depth* to her program with Common Core State Standards where decisions are based on a variety of sources.

Principle One: Walk In, Talk It Out

During this informal observation in Ms. High Stepper's classroom, Mr. Coacher surveys the students about the purposes of the different activities as they relate to cell division and how they will be assessed at the end of the unit. This visit provides the foundation for conversations about assessment during grade-level team meetings.

Observation Focus: Ms. High Stepper is teaching a ninth-grade biology lesson on DNA, cell division, inherited traits, and genetic diseases.

Observation Summary: The teacher sets a context for the DNA lesson with students, which discusses dominant and recessive genes. All twenty-eight ninth graders watch as she demonstrates that she cannot roll her tongue. She tells them, "We are looking at inherited traits as determined by our DNA and what sometimes happens when a genetic disorder occurs. In this lab, we will accomplish three tasks. With the multiple goals for today, you will be able to cooperatively demonstrate your understanding of cell division, apply personal information to a simulation of your offspring's traits, and continue your research on the genetic disease you selected to study." The teacher asks students to go to their assigned areas at the tables or to the computer lab stations.

Students quickly reorganize in their preassigned areas and, after several scurried interactions, settle into the preparations for their prescribed tasks. The teacher talks privately with two girls who are about to use a computer program to plot their inherited traits using personal charts they developed.

The students at the tables create large diagrams on poster paper. They roll different colors of modeling clay into small cylinders, illustrating human cells, and proceed to chart the process of cell division. All seem engaged in the learning as the teacher monitors and coaches the cooperative teams appropriately.

At the same time, one pair in the computer lab logs onto the pedigree program and begin plotting their facial features based on their data.

Principle Two: Align Lessons to the CCSS

Mr. Coacher looks for application of the Common Core literacy standards for science in the lesson. He knows that these standards may require content subject teachers to make adjustments in their instructional approach.

Observation Focus: Students will be able to demonstrate the concept of cell division. Students will be able to plot their pedigree of inherited traits. Students will be able to research a genetic disease and report on the findings from text sources and online interviews, orally and in writing.

Observation Summary: The lesson focused on Reading Standards for Literacy in Science and Technical Subjects. The standards are the following.

Domain: Integration of Knowledge and Ideas

RST.9–10.7: Translate quantitative or technical information expressed in words in a text into visual form (for example, a table or chart) and translate information expressed visually or mathematically (for example, in an equation) into words.

Domain: Key Ideas and Details

RST.9–10.3: Follow precisely a complex multistep procedure when carrying out experiments, taking measurements, or performing technical tasks, attending to special cases or exceptions defined in the text.

RST.9–10.1: Cite specific textual evidence to support analysis of science and technical texts, attending to the precise details of explanations or descriptions. (NGA & CCSSO, 2010a, p. 62)

Principle Three: Facilitate Coaching Conversations

Mr. Coacher identifies seven questions to organize the coaching conversations. The questions focus on CCSS alignment, lesson development, student engagement, and text complexity.

Observation Focus 1: How is the task aligned to the CCSS?

Observation Summary 1: Alignment is clear and appropriate in all three tasks because the assignment directly focuses on rigor, application, and assessment of an understanding of the problem through oral and written explanations.

Observation Focus 2: How is the lesson a part of a unit?

Observation Summary 2: The three parts of this biology lesson on the DNA unit address three critical elements and how they are related: (1) cell division, (2) inherited traits, and (3) genetic diseases.

Observation Focus 3: What did you want students to be able to do at the end of the lesson?

Observation Summary 3: The teacher identifies a multistep process at the beginning of the lesson that is engaging and authentic.

While students understand the task, the clear criterion for proficiency is not mentioned. The teacher misses the opportunity to tell the students about the expectations for writing, speaking, listening, and using technology skills in their research with sources and families in their assignment on genetic diseases. This lesson spans across science and literacy standards, and it is important to make those connections explicit for students.

Observation Focus 4: Are you creating, developing, or enriching curious students by focusing on the process and not the answer?

Observation Summary 4: Students use technology skills, as well as reading, writing, and communication skills in collaborative settings. Students use their scientific knowledge and strategic skills to demonstrate, produce, and research. They also construct a viable model of cell division with an oral explanation of what is occurring, develop a computer model of their pedigree, and report their findings on a genetic condition in writing and in an oral presentation.

Observation Focus 5: Does the task require students to think and use information from the text?

Observation Summary 5: The task requires students to demonstrate understanding of the text for the process of mitosis, as well as develop a chart of inherited traits to apply to the computerized image. In addition, they have to think about what questions to ask their families in their interviews and letters about the genetic disease under study.

Observation Focus 6: How do students know when they're successful? Can all learners succeed?

Observation Summary 6: There are multiple steps for students to complete in this lesson and products that include charts, reports, and performances. However, the teacher did not share an explicit grading plan with students.

Observation Focus 7: Are the texts at the appropriate level of complexity for the grade?

Observation Summary 7: The texts are grade-level appropriate and are suitable for knowledge acquisition. The CCSS specifically state the following.

> **RST.9–10.10:** By the end of grade 10, read and comprehend science and technical texts in the grades 9–10 text complexity band independently and proficiently. (NGA & CCSSO, 2010b, p. 62)

Principle Four: Invite Me Back

Mr. Coacher reminds Ms. High Stepper about his observation that she didn't include a grading plan as part of the lesson (see Observation Summary 6 in principle three). They agree that students were engaged and knew the purpose of each activity; however, they were not sure how they would be evaluated.

Observation Focus: How do students know when they're successful? Can all students learn?

Observation Summary: The teacher decides to develop a performance task grading tool (table 4.3) for presentations with the students as they prepared to finalize their presentation materials on genetic diseases.

The students use the rubric to determine the quality of their work, and then they engage in a 3-2-1 peer review. Students are required to write *three* unique qualities assessed, *two* questions about the work, and *one* suggestion for improving the assignment. The group discussion is rich and relevant. It allows all learners a chance to examine their work, compare the quality of their work, and improve what they have done.

Table 4.3: Ms. High Stepper's Performance Task Grading Tool

Criterion	Developing	Meeting	Exceeding
Given models, students can demonstrate cell division, inherited traits and pedigrees, and the role of genetic disorders as they study the DNA unit.	Students can create models with guidance to describe cell division, inherited traits, and genetic disorders.	Students can show the process of mitosis, using models to develop a chart of inherited traits cooperatively, and begin the research process with a partner. Students will write about their discoveries.	Students can explain cell division efficiently, extrapolate the pedigree, and chart and draw the results. Students can write about the discoveries and give additional instances using real-life examples.

Principle Five: Have Data-Informed Peer Conversations

Together, Mr. Coacher and Ms. High Stepper identify resources she will share with her team at its next meeting. The criteria in her performance task grading tool are consistent with the Common Core literacy standards for academic language and understanding complex text.

Observation Focus: What will the teacher bring to discuss at the grade-level team meeting?

- Evidence of improvement from using the performance task grading tool (student-work samples)
- Reflection from the informal observations of student performance

Observation Summary: The teacher shares the three parts of the lesson and how she utilizes various workstations to actively engage students in the DNA lesson with concrete, representational, and abstract components to clarify, deepen, and apply the learning in real-world and relevant experiences.

The teacher is able to look at what the students need to *understand, know*, and *do* to complete the assignment.

- **Understand:** Students use photos of the graphic organizers and modeling clay activity, computer images of the various pedigrees developed, and research reports on the genetic diseases.

- **Know:** Students learned discipline-specific vocabulary words, including *DNA, mitosis, genetics, pedigree*, and *disease*.

- **Do:** Students' family interviews on inherited traits including eye and hair color were assignments that students had to do at home as part of their real-world learning experience.

Looking Back

Preparing students for college and careers is the main focus of the Common Core State Standards. Effective leaders engage in examining the major changes that transform teaching and learning. These changes include:

- All performance tasks are clearly stated and aligned to the CCSS.

- All lessons are a part of a unit that allows for regular practice.

- All instruction is focused on complex text with use of explicit textual support.

- All students engage in writing across disciplines as a comprehension strategy.

- All students are able to participate fully and succeed.

Although there are fewer standards, the standards are rigorous and coherent with increasing text complexity. As a building leader visits classrooms, he or she thinks about what will allow the informal observations to move into rich, meaningful discussions about improving teaching and learning. The best principals know that planning plus preparation equals success.

Discussion Questions

The discussion questions are for collaborative, grade-level, or department teams or even just two colleagues working together or with a principal as part of a staff meeting to discuss this chapter as part of a book study or as a stand-alone chapter with good information and examples for rigorous and relevant learning. There is nothing as powerful as reflective conversation among professionals.

1. What other Common Core State Standards could the teacher include in the fifth-grade prediction lesson? Provide specific reasons for your selection.

2. How will your school ensure that teachers use reading material with a range of text complexity?

3. Discuss the difference between simple text support and complex text support.

4. The phrase "a mile wide, but only an inch deep" describes the nature of mathematics instruction in the United States. How are the CCSS designed to overcome this limitation?

Takeaways

In a final look back, consider the following takeaways for this chapter. These are just some of the learnings that will benefit you as you support, observe, and evaluate great instruction.

- Visit classrooms often

- Observe and take notes

- Focus on teacher and student moves

- Align the lesson to the Common Core

- Facilitate coaching conversations for reflection

- Make meaningful suggestions and recommendations

- Utilize the Invite Me Back strategy for planned instructional changes and practice

- Develop mobile data walls that incorporate summative and formative facts

CHAPTER 5

The Shift in Assessing Results

Informing All Stakeholders

The most important things we need to manage can't be measured.

—W. Edwards Deming

At Manor New Technology High School in Manor, Texas, the principal is in the driver's seat driving Miss Data. Since 2007, this school's scores have climbed steadily upward. By 2011, a 50 percent free-and-reduced lunch, diverse student population has outperformed the state of Texas and Manor Independent School District in the percentage of students passing state standards in three of the four subjects tested on the Texas Assessment of Knowledge and Skills (TAKS). The English and social studies scores are at 95 percent, mathematics scores are at 71 percent, and science scores are at 86 percent.

"We are a data-driven school," Principal Steve Zipkes commented. "Some would say we are obsessive, but data give us the information for reaching our goals. We have 100 percent of our students going to college, no dropouts, and now the entire district wants to copy our style. When compared to the rest of the state, the results are even more awesome."

When Jim Bellanca visited the school in 2010 and discussed the achievements, Principal Steve Zipkes said, "We decided to act on the mathematics gap. . . . None of us were happy with the mathematics scores. In four years since we started this 100 percent project-based learning and STEM school, our kids have surpassed our goals in every subject but mathematics, and the achievement gap for our African American and Hispanic students was especially worrisome.

"After our faculty analyzed the TAKS numbers, we went to the formative information we had. We wanted to pinpoint some causes. Then, we took a big leap. We gathered our kids together and asked them to add their ideas on both the problem and the solution. It was a very frank talk and one we would have to act on if we were to keep our relationship with them. These were the most important data we collected . . . and the results speak loudest."

"What happened?" Jim asked.

"It's a public record. We worked to change how we taught. We had gaps to fill. As a result, we topped off our schoolwide mathematics scores with 91 percent on the TAKS. The African American students jumped a remarkable 42 points to 86 percent, meeting standards with a gap closure of 38 points. Our Hispanic students jumped up 18 points with a 91 percent score that closed the mathematics gap 8 points.

"Everyone must be pleased," Jim commented.

"Pleased, yes. Complacent, no!" Principal Zipkes responded.

"What do you plan to do now?"

Principal Zipkes didn't hesitate. "Do more data work. We still have some goals to reach."

Principal Zipkes doesn't stand alone in his approach to improving student performance and using an approach that starts with an innovative mindset that acknowledges there is a rock in the road. Rather than trying to roll the rock aside himself, he calls on his faculty members to use their problem-solving talents in a collaborative effort. Shared leadership drives the practices of continuous improvement. The success of shared leadership is evident in the work of such schools as the Denver Green School public charter, the Project Schools in Indiana, Claremont Academy Elementary School in Chicago, the Envision Schools in California, and many other schools in the Deeper Learning Network (www.hewlett.org/deeperlearning). These school leaders understand that their successes in rock rolling don't stop with removal of one or two rocks from the improvement road. They understand that they will need the full strength of their faculty, and, sometimes as happened at Manor Independent School District, their students.

The Continuous-Improvement Buzz

The term *continuous improvement* has buzzed through education and business circles since the days of W. Edwards Deming (1982) and his introduction of quality control to the U.S. auto industry. Few school districts have captured the spirit of Deming's data-driven decision making of many of the schools in the Deeper Learning Network. For their leaders, the phrase *results matter* resonates with school and district leaders as they use assessment as the collaborative tool to find the best practices to most help their students garner a rich and rigorous 21st century education.

Since 2007, principal Steve Zipkes and the Manor New Tech faculty have pushed the improvement envelope by gathering, analyzing, and acting on the best data they could find. Each year, they make refinements as they risk one innovation after another to ensure that every student exceeds the new expectations. Even as their schoolwide achievement test scores rise, the faculty is not happy with the continued math achievement gap that stands out like a sore thumb.

In best practice research, engagement of multiple stakeholders for innovative school improvement has taken a backseat. However, a 2012 study from the Northwest Evaluation Association (NWEA) adds significantly to the assessment picture. The study is especially important because it argues for the inclusion of all stakeholders' views, including those of parents, and compares those data to the views of teachers and administrators.

All three groups surveyed agree on a single top-priority need. The study shows that assessment information first and foremost should inform multiple constituencies about individual student progress and decisions to improve instruction and school-wide results. The groups ask that this information come from multiple sources and provide multiple points of view that could inform everyday teaching and learning. As a second priority, all groups want to see summative information either through standardized test results or end-of-course subject exams that could fuel schoolwide improvements. Intermingled with these priorities is a shared insistence on the dual importance of measuring student performance in a full range of subjects along with thinking skills that will be critical in life (NWEA, 2012).

This study provides a starting point for examining the instructional leader's role in the multifaceted assessment tasks of a 21st century standards–aligned school. As noted in the Manor New Tech example, principals play an important role in leading the schools' collaborative assessment policies and procedures. Think of principals' multiple roles as hats on a hat rack, two of which are connected to assessment considerations. The first is the hat they wear when managing the school's overall student performance. The principal takes the second hat from the rack when developing teacher performance in pursuit of those same schoolwide improvement goals. Principals on top of their game know that these two hats hang on the same rack, sometimes needing separation, but best kept near each other in a systematic, connected framework that ultimately guides teachers to data decisions about every student in their classrooms.

A principal's first hat, the Sunday go-to-meeting hat, is the most important for instructional leaders because it represents schoolwide student performance. In 21st century schools, that hat bears two feathers of equal size and attractiveness: the achievement feather and the process skills feather. A second hat represents another area important to principals—teacher performance. Figure 5.1 illustrates these two aspects of a principal's leadership responsibilities.

Figure 5.1: Principal's responsibilities for overseeing assessment practices.

Innovative principals engage their leadership teams so as to give equal care to noting how well the students in each class and the school as a whole are improving. They do so by putting the interpretation of that data into action that continues the cyclical and balanced three-phase improvement process. The phases of this process are (1) gathering information, (2) analyzing information, and (3) acting on information. We describe these phases using our driving Miss Data metaphor to emphasize the reality of assessment challenges in school.

Phase One: Gathering Information With Miss Data

Each year, principals put on the Sunday go-to-meeting hat as soon as they begin the first phase of the continuous assessment process. Because they delegate the formative and interim assessments of students to their teachers, innovative principals are free to focus on how well their teachers know and use a variety of data to fill each student's performance portfolio. The more information that teachers assemble about a student's past school performance, culture, family conditions, mental and physical health, and well-being, the more effective they can be in ensuring that they meet each student's full range of needs. Some of the data comes from school records, some from conversations with parents and former teachers, and some from watching, listening, and talking to students themselves. With this foundation, teachers are free to focus fully on their primary goal, the factor teachers and parents most desire according to the NWEA (2012) study: assurance that each and every student makes the maximum possible gains in academic performance and development of life skills.

The principal's second hat looks much like the first. It too has two feathers: one for achievement (content) and one for thinking-skills development. Principals put this hat on each time they or their delegates visit classrooms to observe teachers. It reminds them that the primary focus of this collaborative visit is balanced observation of how the teacher is impacting student learning while simultaneously developing the 21st century process skills—critical thinking, problem solving, and collaboration skills embedded in the standards. The collaborative visits enable teachers to provide constructive feedback on the progress of their plan to improve performance of all students.

Using Multiple Sources, Multiple Views

To ensure that all students are moving toward balanced development of the knowledge and skills highlighted in the CCSS, school leaders direct the school team in collecting, analyzing, and using data to inform decisions that teachers can implement to improve individual, grade-level, and schoolwide performance results. The data come from multiple sources, which require that school leaders pull the multiple pieces together and seize the advantage of multiple views in all phases of the assessment cycle.

The generic word *data* can lead to many disagreements in interpretation and purpose. In the context of the CCSS, data are those information sources that best assist the principal and school team to make robust decisions that end in measurable, balanced improvements. Such data must include quantitative numbers gathered from formative quizzes and tests, interim standardized exams, and end-of-year national summative exams.

It is imperative that school teams balance the so-called *hard* numbers with qualitative snapshots—*soft data*—on how students are performing to illustrate how well teachers are impacting both student achievement *and* 21st century skill development. This valuable soft data can include checklists and rubrics applied to classroom observations, teacher notes, student essays and artifacts, photographs, videos, recorded parent feedback, and other documents that provide insight into the quality of student learning. Such data are especially valuable for identifying those aspects of school life and learning that aren't covered in standardized tests' quick-and-narrow snapshots. Table 5.1 (page 126) shows examples of multiple data tools.

Principals have specific responsibilities to lead the school's data-gathering effort. They delegate other responsibilities to teachers. Principals are responsible for guiding the formation of the schoolwide plan, keeping focus on the big assessment picture, improving implementation practices of the standards, monitoring logistics, and communicating results to the faculty, parents, and district. In each of the plan's three assessment phases, different paint strokes color these responsibilities.

Table 5.1: Multiple Data Tools

Quantitative Tools	Qualitative Tools	Qualitative Sources	Qualitative Targets	Qualitative Assessments
Interim test scores	Rubrics	Oral presentations	Collaborative competencies	Student self-assessments
Formative quiz scores	Checklists	Writing samples	Problem-solving competencies	Peer assessments
Student attendance numbers	Complexity graphs	Essays	Critical thinking competencies	Teacher assessments
Student behavior statistics		Goal charts	Creative thinking competencies	Parent assessments
Homework completion counts		Journal entries	Self-directed learning competencies	
Summative test results		Project-based learning plans		
		Project-based learning artifacts		
		Project-based lesson summaries		

Creating the Assessment Plan

On an annual basis, the principal is the guide on the side who facilitates the work of an assessment task force in constructing the assessment plan and delineating responsibilities, timelines, and methods as a part of the school's continuous-improvement effort. The task force's charge is to make the assessment process systematic, coherent, inclusive, and focused so that it makes practical sense for high-impact classroom implementation.

Focused and Coherent

The CCSS ELA/literacy anchor standards for the Reading, Writing, Speaking and Listening, and Language strands (NGA & CCSSO, 2010a) and the CCSS Mathematical Practices (NGA & CCSSO, 2010e) provide the foci for assessment plans and practices in each area. It is the principal's responsibility to keep these foci in mind during classroom observations as well as to help teachers maintain them as the most significant parts of the assessments they do with students. The principal helps teachers connect the dots and maintain a coherent view of the CCSS as they gather data on individual student needs and adjust instruction accordingly. While end-of-unit exams or end-of-year standardized tests in the elementary grades are only pathways to high-stakes high school tests and college entrance exams, the formative and interim exams students face in the elementary grades are stepping stones to what they will encounter in the later grades. The anchor standards and the mathematics proficiencies are the all-important road signs to which the principal constantly calls attention lest anyone makes an accidental errant turn.

Systematic

Principals have to know how well their emphasis on keeping the focus is affecting student performance—helping or hindering it. School leaders need a practical tool to help organize data collected from lesson plans, test and rubric samples, teacher observation checklists from walkthroughs, and other artifacts. Kidblog (www.kidblog.org) is a tool that provides a practical solution. By signing into this free blog, the principal can create private miniblogs for each teacher. Guided by a collaborative rubric, the principal and the teacher can both enter selected materials. With pin-coded control which provides security and privacy, the two can confer in the miniblog space. The reproducible "Evaluating Blog Data" (page 146) is a tool for determining the effectiveness of the entries in the miniblog.

Information the principal obtains from classroom observation walkthroughs (see chapter 4, pages 99–118) augments data gathered from individual teachers in other circumstances. The classroom observations provide the most authentic information that the principal can use for coaching and feedback conversations with teachers. At least half the notes the principal takes during a walkthrough should capture how teachers are focusing on the anchor standards or Mathematical Practices to guide student learning. Principals' looks-likes charts provide the essential balance given to standards-aligned instruction by capturing evidence that reasoning and problem solving are receiving as much attention as the content elements of the lesson target (see chapter 3). Furthermore, the principal needs to look for evidence that the teacher is using the highest-impact instructional strategies to help students maintain that dual focus. When the principal observes gaps or *bird walks* in the lesson, he or she needs to identify the gap and assist the teacher in adjusting practice so that the teacher does not stray from the lesson's focus. That responsibility, however, doesn't end with the feedback. By maintaining a positive relationship with the teacher, the leader gets the invited callbacks to see how the teacher has adopted the advice.

Focusing instruction on the Mathematical Practices and ELA/literacy anchor standards is necessary every day in each classroom. However, that alone is not sufficient to achieve the largest gains in student performance. For many teachers, the multiple switches the CCSS present necessitate multiple switches in instruction and assessment that may well be outside their comfort zone and often their knowledge zone. The principal's sharp eyes and ears will capture instances of gaps in teacher performance that may be limiting students' peak performances as well as where students may be outside their comfort and knowledge zones. Through repeated walkthroughs, these active leaders will note areas needing attention and provide constructive feedback on the teacher's progress.

Assessing Instructional Proficiencies

The CCSS shifts in instruction lead to shifts in assessment practices. At the national level, the PARCC and SBAC assessments will drive the shifts in formative and interim assessments. In turn, instruction will change. By examining these assessments to see what they are asking students to know and do, instructional leaders have a strong starting point for framing observations and conversations with teachers about data collection. The results of these dialogues will have a major impact on the school's improvement results especially when the assessments reveal observable student performances and their results. For example, a checklist or rubric that focuses the principal's eye on how students are building a worm compost bin or how precisely they are taking measurements to build a room goes hand in hand with how the completed bin or the built room matches the criteria for the task.

Quality of instruction drives student performance (Chetty, Freidman, & Rockoff, 2011). Principals have the task of helping teachers shape their instruction to help students understand content and develop the skills identified in the standards. For instance, the Common Core summative assessments for English language arts examine students' ability to analyze multiple texts and write synthesizing persuasive essays to show reasoning. When teachers adapt their qualitative summative rubrics to serve also as their formative tools, they highlight the development of students' process skills leading to deeper learning outcomes. Therefore, it is only logical that the school plan provide evidence that grade-level teachers are indeed teaching the writing skills in the CCSS and that the writing tasks require students to produce persuasive pieces that synthesize ideas and capture the reasoning in materials analyzed. Multiple data sources that capture students' development as thinkers in this more complex task can include rubrics to guide assessment of student artifacts, observations of teachers using strategies that guide students' skill development, and multiple-view assessments including students' self-assessments that show progress as they build, write, draw, design, or perform.

Likewise in mathematics, school or department leaders can listen to students' guided discussions about problem solving and observe collaborative groups using graphic representations, making charts, and hypothesizing to solve equations. While the students are participating in this kind of high-effects instruction, the leader can concentrate on what the teacher says and does to facilitate quality reasoning, idea generation, and problem selection, especially for low performers. By observing both student and teacher behaviors, the school leader has ample clues from which to formulate inferences that tie how students are solving problems and understanding mathematical concepts to the teachers' skillful adoption of strategies that prompt these results.

In the 21st century, what makes for quality instruction requires no guessing game. Research makes clear which instructional strategies and which programs most impact achievement, which develop problem-solving proficiencies, and which do both in one fell swoop (Afflerbach, Pearson, & Paris, 2008; Allington, 2011; Brenner & Hiebert, 2010; Hattie, 2009). If teachers need assistance to include additional best practices to their repertoires, effective school leaders behave like surgeons in the best hospitals: both move heaven and earth to see that their professional staff develop their best practice skills and continuously search out ways to foster improvement.

As instructional supervisors observe teachers using sound instructional practices—explicit instruction of thinking skills, close reading of text, concept-rich mathematics instruction, and inquiry learning—they can take note of the extent to which teachers are continuously upgrading their instructional proficiencies with appropriate research-based strategies. Using a stepladder graphic (see figure 5.2, page 130), a principal observer may note how a competent teacher selects high-effects strategies that most correlate with higher achievement and fit the lesson to increase the effect-size possibilities. Perhaps the teacher combines cooperative learning with graphic organizers and hypothesis testing integrated with an inquiry into Huck Finn's adventures. Perhaps the mathematics teacher supplies differentiated student teams each with a different set of manipulatives, symbols, and visuals for solving a mathematics problem. Both indicate high degrees of teaching competency.

Using the stepladder graphic, school leaders can record how a teacher has advanced his or her strategies to encompass more complex approaches such as project-based learning integrated with technology and organized minilabs for explicit instruction of key thinking skills. For example, the leader would be able to collect evidence by watching students work in collaborative teams to frame an essential question about water pollution in local streams or how modern hometown heroes compare with Greek heroes. Seeing students do online research with a SurveyMonkey (www .surveymonkey.com) questionnaire and watching the teacher move among the teams to listen and frame "Why are you selecting that?" questions, the observer notes the clues that suggest, "These kids aren't doing this by accident" and jots a note-to-self reminder, "Ask Ms. High Stepper what she did to prepare their research skills. These kids are awesome investigators."

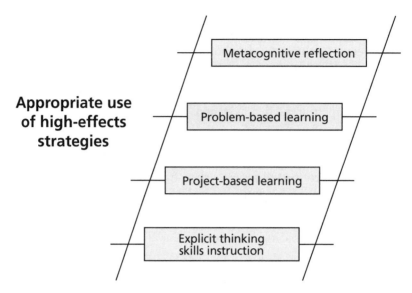

Figure 5.2: The stepladder of instructional proficiency.

*Visit **go.solution-tree.com/leadership** for a reproducible version of this figure.*

At the most challenging instructional proficiency level, the principal can record how well a teacher employs metacognitive strategies to deepen student reflections and self-assessment. For instance, in a cross-curricular reading task that involves science and social studies articles, the principal is ready with a self-made observation rubric that will enable him or her to record how the teacher sets up a culture for reflection, prompts students to think about their thinking, and encourages students to provide evidence from their readings and discussions that make their responses most meaningful. Questions such as these can guide the principal's observations.

- What guiding questions does the teacher ask?
- What probing questions does the teacher ask?
- How appropriate are the evaluation questions?

Figure 5.3 is an example of an observation rubric that a principal can use to observe students' metacognitive activity while a teacher engages students in reflection and assessment tasks.

A crucial part of the principal's observation and feedback is the students' self-assessment rubric (see figure 5.4, page 132) that the teacher had prepared and discussed with the principal. Like other process rubrics, this metacognition rubric would guide the students' development of their self-assessment skill over time. It was not a one-shot effort. In addition, the teacher's decision to introduce metacognition into her instructional repertoire marked her readiness to accept the highest challenge for deeper learning instruction. Not only would she prompt her students to think about

Teacher: Ann Heinz   **Date:** April 25   **Period:** 3

Reason for observation: Candidate for Level 3:—Setting up project reflection that includes students thinking about their reasoning process and their collaboration.

Unit or lesson: What's With Our Water? **Standards:** RI.8.2–3, SL.8.1

Teacher-requested focus: Engaging students in meaningful metacognitive reflection and assessment

Scale: 0 (not yet) to 5 (exceptional performance)

Teacher Actions	Teacher Action Rating	Student Responses	Student Engagement Rating
Set up groups	5	Prompt move	5
Facilitated roles and responsibilities	5	Prompt response	4.5
Presented student open-ended self-reflection rubrics	5	Prompt agreement	5
Identified target process skills for critical thinking and collaboration	4	Asked for clarification	5
Checked for understanding	4	Most positive responses	5
Wait time	5	Stirred questions	5
Provided reasons for process skills	5	Student comfort	5
Reviewed criteria for evidence of metacognition	4	Stirred clarification	3
Gave encouragement	3	Two concerned expressions	2
Set time limit	0	Created off-task buzz	0
Added sample	4	Most heads nodded	4
Observed groups	3	Some wait and got off task	2
Coached on response	3	Two groups finished in half the time	2

Pluses: Set up of reflection with tools and tips to students

Questions to ask: Why rush when giving encouragement? Where were time limit and sample? What bogged you down in coaching?

Closure: What do you intend to do differently?

Figure 5.3: Sample tool for observing metacognitive activity.

*Visit **go.solution-tree.com/leadership** for a reproducible version of this figure.*

Students: Thom Anderson, Megan O'Reilly, and Jason Parker **Date:** March 13

Class: Biology 12   **Period:** 3–4   **Unit:** Genome Project   **Teacher:** Donna Menendez

Focus Reasoning Skill: Problem Definition

Self-Assessment Criteria	Not Yet	Getting There	Good Shape	The Ultimate
To what degree does your reflection start with your own definition of the reasoning skill selected?				
To what degree does your reflection assess this mental menu by assessing criteria and/or providing support to: • Describe the problem? • Evidence the description from the data? • Fine tune the problem statement? • Investigate ways the character would define the problem? • Note additional evidence data? • Evaluate degree that the refined definition is precise and accurate?				
To what degree does your reflection provide examples of pluses and/or minuses about this skill's application in this project?				
To what degree does your reflection provide self-suggestions for improving the skill?				

Figure 5.4: Sample rubric for student self-assessment of metacognition.

Source: Adapted from Bellanca, 2013.

*Visit **go.solution-tree.com/leadership** for a reproducible version of this figure.*

their thinking with a series of open-ended, thought-provoking questions, she would be finding data in their reflective assessments that would allow her to give them the highest-level feedback on how they were developing as thinkers and collaborative problem solvers with the course content.

Assessing and giving helpful, constructive feedback on instructional proficiencies is an important aspect of the principal's role in providing leadership within the school's assessment plan. He or she has to make efficient use of available time and opportunities to observe how teachers adopt strategies and approaches at increased levels of challenge while simultaneously noting the effects on students. In so doing, the principal gains a four-fold payoff.

1. The observational data of teachers in action provide concrete examples that can be used to help teachers continuously refine their knowledge and practice.

2. The observational data of the impact instructional approaches have on students provide information that fills in the blanks about student learning that tests and quizzes cannot provide.

3. These multiple data sources provide fuel for teacher teams as they engage in collegial schoolwide improvement efforts as well as efforts to link their individual improvements to improvements in student performance.

4. The data provide evidence of the probability that teachers who are able to work consistently at the highest levels of instruction will produce the most dramatic double-digit achievement results on individual students as well as on grade-level and schoolwide performance.

Phase Two: Analyzing Information With Miss Data

Gathered data are helpful for planning only when they are filtered and analyzed with precision and accuracy as soon after the collection as possible. School leaders have the responsibility of supporting teachers as they collaboratively deconstruct and reconstruct information from the multiple data sources in phase one of a continuous-improvement process. In phase two, leaders are prepared with tools to analyze data from their own observations, teacher observations of students, quantitative test numbers, and other qualitative information. Three tools stand out as most helpful for the school leaders' 21st century assessment analysis kit: (1) fishbone analysis, (2) gap analysis, and (3) root-cause analysis.

Fishbone Analysis

Kaoru Ishikawa's (1985) fishbone diagram is a cause-and-effect tool used for quality control like product design and car defect prevention. By examining all the factors that might contribute to an effect, such as smeared paint on a car door or an erratic turn signal, car designers could perfect a model line. Similarly, educators can use this approach as they analyze data. The fishbone diagram enables collaborative teams to organize data in ways to eliminate a behavior problem or to raise achievement in a specific strand or skill, such as writing a persuasive essay.

Every fishbone has six possible causes to analyze to reach the effect.

1. **People:** Identify anyone involved in the problem. This category could be broken into subsections for students, parents, teachers, administrators, non-academic personnel, and so on.

2. **Methods:** Identify the policies, practices, and procedures that impact a problem.

3. **Equipment:** Specify whatever tools or equipment are needed to complete the task, such as computers, printers, whiteboards, desks, chairs, water fountains, and playground equipment.

4. **Materials:** Specify classroom supplies, including paper, textbooks, software, teacher guides, and library books.

5. **Environment:** Define the teaching and learning conditions, school culture, or community involvement.

6. **Leadership:** Identify style, engagement, beliefs, knowledge, skills, time, and responsibilities.

As a first step in fishbone analysis, the team (that the principal selects from faculty-generated criteria) agrees on a significant problem that impacts some aspect of school life. That topic identifies the problem to analyze. When the problem is a student issue, the major reason for using a fishbone diagram, the team designates parameters such as "all third graders" or "students in middle-grade basic mathematics." The team can go so far as to identify the Common Core standard involved. Following agreement on the topic, the team identifies the categories of possible causes (*bones*) that connect to the fish head, the problem statement. Figure 5.5 shows one team's analysis of third graders' difficulties in meeting the Reading Informational Text standards, identifying the factors related to solving the problem—people, methods, materials, equipment, environment, and leadership.

After team members chart the possible causes or reasons for students' weak responses, they agree on a common definition of the problem being "students fail to use a systematic approach" and look at the data that indicate sources of the problem.

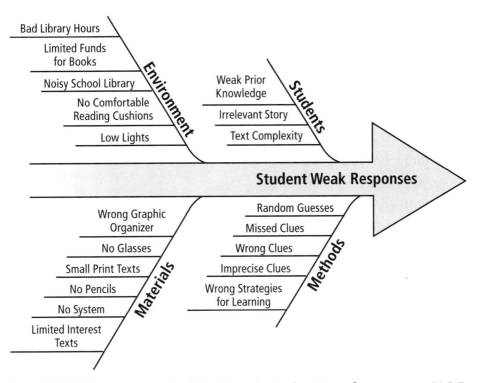

Figure 5.5: Fishbone analysis of third-grade students' performance on RI.3.7.
*Visit **go.solution-tree.com/leadership** for a reproducible version of this figure.*

For example, if teachers chart how many students used the newspaper system with *where*, *when*, *why*, and *how* to determine how many approached the task with a system, data might show the percentage of students who relied on a newspaper graphic, the percentage who made a random list, and the percentage who relied solely on their recall as their reading strategy. Pulling together the students' strategy data, the evidence might show that one teacher uses an observation checklist showing that more than three-quarters of his or her students have no system for picking out the clues and recording ideas precisely. These students simply rely on random memory. Other data may show that some students fell down in one or more areas: 50 percent missed clues, 45 percent picked wrong clues, and 62 percent passed over clues. After the other teachers share their data, the team is ready to move to another form of analysis, such as the gap analysis, or to its plan of action.

Gap Analysis

The simple fishbone diagram is a tool that can guide a team's analyses toward identifying gaps in student performance. For a gap analysis of the problem in figure 5.5, the team would discuss the current state of performance that the data show in contrast to the desired level of performance. Rather than set a desired performance level for a short term only, the team can benchmark percentages of measurable improvement desired by the end of each quarter through the end of the school year. For instance, at the end of the first quarter, the team decides that by the end of the second quarter, 90 percent of students will identify at least 50 percent of text clues and will increase 25 percent for the next two quarters.

There are seven steps to follow when conducting a gap analysis.

1. Identify the existing issue.
2. Identify the current outcome.
3. Identify the desired outcome.
4. Identify the strategies to move to the desired outcome.
5. Break the strategy into components or substeps.
6. Determine the timelines.
7. Determine the measurable behavior.

After defining the desired benchmark percentages, the team turns to planning the how-to process. Noting the low percentage of students using any tool to gather clues and organize them, this team elects to use the newspaper graphic. This organizer contains the five Ws of newspaper writing—who, what, when, where, and why. The teachers use this tool to monitor students as they read and record the clues they find by adopting various strategies. For example, the teacher records "no" for students who didn't use any strategy. Figure 5.6 shows the performance results for seven third-grade students.

In steps five and six of the gap analysis, the team breaks the strategy into steps and sets these into a weekly schedule.

- **Week one:** Team conducts first-round observations with newspaper chart.
- **Week two:** Team conducts second-round observations with newspaper chart.
- **Week three:** Team conducts third-round observations with newspaper chart.
- **Week four:** Individuals analyze charts. Team meets to synthesize results and discuss new strategies.
- **Weeks five, six, and seven:** Team implements new strategies and charts results.
- **Week eight:** Team analyzes results and plans for minilab.

Who	What Strategy	When	Where (text?)	Why
Amanda	web	Tuesday Wednesday	2	character
Ami	X	X	X	X
David	web, sequence	Monday Tuesday Wednesday Thursday	2, 3, 4	character, plot
Raul	web, sequence	Monday Tuesday Wednesday Thursday Friday	1, 3, 3, 4	character, plot
Margery	c-map	Friday	3	theme
Stephanie	X	X	X	X
Tomas	sequence	Friday	2	plot

Figure 5.6: Sample newspaper graphic for RI.3.7.

One important step remains. How are teachers going to ensure that all students make appropriate connections between the clues identified and the occurrence of a key event? What will they do for those students who continue to reject suggestions for using the strategic reading tools? For this, they plan for an explicit instruction minilab. In the classroom minilab, a teacher pulls the students who are still struggling aside while the other students continue with their reading tasks. The teacher will engage the selected students in the first level of the explicit instruction model (see chapter 3, pages 60–70).

The instructional phase of this explicit lesson requires no more than thirty minutes of differentiated instruction. On the following day, the teacher can continue attending to this minilab group by walking through a guided practice with a grade-appropriate text, directing the students to use a web or the newspaper chart to gather information about the main character. After monitoring the group and checking for individual understanding, the teacher can decide which students need additional guided practice and feedback and which are ready to return to independent tasks.

Root-Cause Analysis

Root-cause analysis is more complex than the fishbone analysis. Its complexity springs from the goal of ensuring that the data-analysis process digs down to the root or first cause of the problem. This type of analysis has two parts: (1) asking a series of *why* questions to identify a process that is not working and (2) re-examining the fishbone analysis to gain additional insight into the problem.

The team begins the inquiry with five (or more) *why* questions to identify a process that is not working to its maximum potential. For instance, a middle school's data on dropouts showed a hockey stick jump—a standard statistical image in the shape of a hockey stick—from an annual rate of less than 1 percent per month for the first seven years. In grade 8, the number escalated to more than 2 percent per month peaking in May at 6 percent.

The middle school team's inquiry took the investigators beneath simple, surface questions and answers. Note the increased refinement the questions provide.

1. **What is not working?** Eighth graders are graduating in very limited numbers.

2. **What do the statistics tell us?** There is a 12 percent plus dropout rate in grade 8.

3. **Why?** Forty-five percent of students who drop out say school is boring.

4. **Why?** Eighty-two percent of bored students are failing one or more courses.

5. **Why?** Seventy-eight percent of bored students are failing math.

6. **Why?** Sixty-seven percent of bored students say, "I don't understand prealgebra."

7. **Why?** Eighty-nine percent of bored students say, "I don't see how at least one operation (+, −, ×, ÷) changes in an algorithm."

8. **Why?** One student explains, "I always memorized how to use the numbers, and the algorithms were too hard to memorize" Sixty-two percent reiterated this position as their first selection.

Root-cause analysis is a valuable tool for defining apparent problems by moving beyond (or below) the superficial symptoms. It helps create driving questions for teams because it forces the collection of data that often do not appear and avoids the temptation of quick solutions based on incomplete data. It also suggests that there may be many deep causes hidden from immediate view that are contributing to the problem.

Data analysis that focuses on finding the root causes of common shortages in relation to expected skill and knowledge development sits at the center of closing achievement gaps and developing the learning-to-learn thinking and collaborating skills important for students who will be living and working in a 21st century global economy. Innovative principals facilitate the investigations that help teachers identify evidence-based research strategies that strengthen student learning and solve other problems that hinder student success. By relying on well-established data study strategies such as the root-cause analysis, school teams are able to collaborate around meaningful issues in a systematic way.

Phase Three: Acting on Information With Miss Data

Data collection and analysis without data-supported action waste time and money and kill teacher motivation. The same can be said for taking actions that are simple repeats of the same old sins of the past. By insisting on skillful analyses of what-works data, effective principals take responsibility for leading the school teams in search of solutions. These principals refuse to copycat what hasn't been working or sugarcoat failed practice. This means that school teams have an obligation to seek out data-supported best practices that may carry the school on a new pathway toward a solution to a critically examined problem.

Creative Thinking

Although *data analysis* primarily occurs in the left side of the brain with statistics and probability knowledge, *data action* mostly occurs on the right side. Once the team has analyzed the data and identified the problem, it is important for the principal and team to switch hemispheres and adopt thinking skills to develop innovative, out-of-the-box actions to eliminate the root cause. It is here that principals will do best by resurrecting the image of Leonardo da Vinci, the innovative inventor who sought solutions that were not warmed-over versions, imitations, regurgitations, or replications (see page 15).

The CCSS and 21st century skills create rich opportunities for innovative responses to achievement and skill-development issues that have been holding students back. Each time school leaders are called on to facilitate data-based decisions, opportunities exist to look outside the box at the plethora of data-strong solutions that are alternatives to the outmoded and obsolete approaches of the factory school model. The innovative thinking begins with the skill of generating alternatives in possibility thinking. As Sidney Parnes, Ruth Noller, and Angelo Biondi (1977) note, *brainstorming* is the basic tool for innovative thinking. However, in the 21st century, brainstorming may seem old hat. As old hat as it may appear, when used well, brainstorming has powerful effects.

Brainstorming is a way of thinking that follows guidelines, but prejudgments or negative critiques do not constrain it. Collaboration guidelines encourage individuals and teams to respond to a data-based root cause (for example, "Students in prealgebra haven't learned how to reason") with an essential or root question (such as, "How do I advance the practices of mathematics teachers so they can help students reason more skillfully and solve problems?").

Collaboration Guidelines

Collaborative discussions about student performance problems or other school-based issues can produce lengthy lists or a spider web of possible solutions. As facilitators, school leaders can add their own ideas and build on team members' contributions. It is important to follow an agreed-on set of team guidelines during collaborative discussions, such as ALL ROW in figure 5.7.

A = Assist each other to attain the same goal.

L = Link everyone's talents.

L = Leverage all ideas.

R = Recognize the smallest contributions.

O = Obtain the strongest agreements.

W = Work for win-win for all.

Figure 5.7: Sample collaborative discussion guidelines.

*Visit **go.solution-tree.com/leadership** for a reproducible version of this figure.*

The idea-generating process begins with the team jigsawing a search of best practice information that will help answer a question. This is an open-ended search to find possible answers to an open-ended question. No sure-to-be-right, presupposed answers are acceptable. For example, googling *middle school math, understanding of algorithms* brings up many results. Consequently, the team has to filter the items using such criteria as publication date, citations, source reliability, specific response to the question, credibility of authors, and research support. As a result of this screening, the team selects, distributes, summarizes, and discusses appropriate articles—those that can be used to answer the driving question.

After team members have read the articles, the brainstorming begins. Teams thrive on adding to, modifying, cutting down, dividing, expanding, or altering ideas they've generated per their reading and prior experience. The team can decide on how many items will remain on the final list. For making a selection, teams may use majority vote, highest total point score, or another numerical selector that meets the team's agreed-on criteria. Teams can build these criteria using the same brainstorming and selection strategy. The criteria list works best in response to the open-ended lead-in question: To what degree do we think this solution—

- Will impact all students?
- Is measurable?
- Is innovative?
- Has a strong research or evidence base?
- Is possible to implement?
- Is legal?
- Has the strongest likely result?
- Is affordable?

Goal Setting and Review

Once the team has selected resources that best match the criteria, the principal calls for one or two volunteers to write an ABC goal statement that shows the goal is achievable, believable, and compatible.

- **Achievable:** With this criterion, team members recognize specific, measurable results that define the outcomes so that they can say, "We believe that we can accomplish this goal and see specific results in a set amount of time."
- **Believable:** With this criterion, team members are able to assert their passionate commitment to carrying out the tasks that show there is a high degree of probability that they can get the results they desire. "Yes, we can do this."
- **Compatible:** With this criterion, the team notes that the plan's goals and actions fit with the values of the school and community. With that understanding, team members are ready to declare that there is substantial and substantive agreement that the practices they've selected are in the best interests of the students and deserve a trial.

The goal statement presents a solution that meets the criteria and is based on new ideas for addressing the achievement problem.

In the final steps, the principal facilitates the implementation of concrete actions, timelines, products, staff responsibilities, and evaluation. In this sample action plan, the ingredients respond to a goal that addresses the root cause of the problem the team identified (see figure 5.8, page 143). The task force members jigsaw specific responsibilities and create checkpoints for continuous data collection.

Action plans are important documents in the improvement effort. When facilitated carefully by an innovative principal, the time spent builds collaborative relations among the professionals and leads to a strengthened, purposeful learning community. With an action plan, the school team has a guide for action, a tool for assessment, and

Goal: Reduce the eighth-grade dropout rate from 12 percent per year by half each year for the next three years (to 6 percent, 3 percent, and 1.5 percent).		
Actions	**Monitors From Task Force**	**Review Date**
1. Schedule dual-period mathematics. Block in grades 6–8	Principal: Al Smith	September 1
2. Prepare teachers with standards-aligned cognitive mathematics each year one period per day.	Monica Diaz and Jasmine Smith	August 15–19
3. Prepare teachers with critical-thinking program one period per day, grades 6–8.	Monica Diaz and Jasmine Smith	October 1–2 December 5–6
4. Set up peer support teams grades 6–8 for planning and formative assessments.	Martin Bloethner and Sidney Bush	September 1
5. Collect and assess quarterly data on student progress with control and experimental feedback.	Howard Elias	September 1
6. Set up career and college program with school counselor and volunteers to meet with families at least once annually.	Gregor Rasmussan	August 15
7. Introduce STEM strategies toolbox as an online remediation resource.	Madeline Choco	August 15
8. Review data on implementation and results quarterly.	Principal: Al Smith	September 1

Sample Products to Assess

- Classroom visuals for mathematics proficiencies
- Teacher time chart and lessons for problem solving
- Teacher rubrics with student problem-solving tasks
- Teacher rubrics with mathematics or ELA reasoning tasks
- Quarterly interim test results for problem solving
- Observation checklist of reasoning and problem solving
- Peer support teams with assessments of progress
- Parent assessments of college meetings
- Student results data from online tasks

Project Rubric

Title: Expanding Problem Solving in Mathematics

Grades: 6–8   **School:** M. L. King Elementary, District 99

Teachers: Jones, McCandless, and Masterson-Ruiz   **Date:** March 13

To what degree do you have evidence of improvement? Enter percentage of students.

1. Making sense of problem statement

   _____ Not yet   _____ Getting started   _____ Solid grasp   _____ Soaring eagle

2. Forming a problem statement

   _____ Not yet   _____ Getting started   _____ Solid grasp   _____ Soaring eagle

3. Generating alternative ways to solve the problem

   _____ Not yet   _____ Getting started   _____ Solid grasp   _____ Soaring eagle

4. Performing computations with accuracy

   _____ Not yet   _____ Getting started   _____ Solid grasp   _____ Soaring eagle

5. Using precise language and exact terms

   _____ Not yet   _____ Getting started   _____ Solid grasp   _____ Soaring eagle

6. Using tools strategically

   _____ Not yet   _____ Getting started   _____ Solid grasp   _____ Soaring eagle

7. Increasing abstract and quantitative reasoning skills

   _____ Not yet   _____ Getting started   _____ Solid grasp   _____ Soaring eagle

8. Modeling responses

   _____ Not yet   _____ Getting started   _____ Solid grasp   _____ Soaring eagle

9. Reflecting on problem solving

   _____ Not yet   _____ Getting started   _____ Solid grasp   _____ Soaring eagle

Figure 5.8: A sample data-based action plan.

*Visit **go.solution-tree.com/leadership** for a reproducible version of this figure.*

a piece of evidence telling about its systematic efforts to continuously find innovative improvements that benefit all students.

Looking Back

A cycle of continuous assessment encourages school teams to refine their improvement efforts year after year. In 2011, when Manor New Tech High's assessment team examined the state assessment data and disaggregated them by the student populations, it didn't rest on its laurels. The school already had double achievement scores across the board but its mathematics results hadn't yet arrived for two of its populations. More data collection, including student ideas, drove the next cycle of planning to get at the root causes of the achievement gap. New strategies emerged. Teachers and students gave new effort and voila!—another giant step!

"But only one step," commented principal Steve Zipkes in a Skype conversation. "The math scores are not yet where we think they can be. So we won't stop using our data to help us make the next steps."

Discussion Questions

The discussion questions are for collaborative, grade-level, or department teams or even just two colleagues working together or with a principal as part of a staff meeting to discuss this chapter as part of a book study or as a stand-alone chapter with good information and examples for rigorous and relevant learning. There is nothing as powerful as reflective conversation among professionals.

1. What is the value of school leaders believing in continuous improvement?

2. What specific strategies can you add to your data-analysis repertoire that will assist your school teams in making sense of data collected?

3. What arguments can you make for or against the implication that because instructional practices differ in level of difficulty they have different degrees of impact on student learning?

4. How can you strengthen the data cycle in your school so that it makes a greater impact on both teaching and learning?

5. Given the sum total of beliefs, attributes, and competencies identified as essential for an innovative 21st century leader, how do you assess your own proficiency in advancing the Common Core State Standards with your faculty?

Takeaways

In a final look back, consider the following takeaways for this chapter. These are just some of the learnings that will benefit you as you support, observe, and evaluate great instruction.

- Information-gathering checklists
- Data-analysis tools
- Planning rubrics

Evaluating Blog Data

Determine to what degree the entries in the blog do the following.

1. Highlight proficiencies in one or more Mathematical Practices?

   ☐ Not Yet   ☐ Some   ☐ Strong   ☐ Tight

2. Connect to one or more ELA/literacy anchor standards?

   ☐ Not Yet   ☐ Some   ☐ Strong   ☐ Tight

3. Tie an activity to a Mathematical Practice or anchor standard?

   ☐ Not Yet   ☐ Some   ☐ Strong   ☐ Tight

4. Support the Mathematical Practice or anchor standard with thinking skills from the targeted grade-level standards?

   ☐ Not Yet   ☐ Some   ☐ Strong   ☐ Tight

5. Show improvement in making connections to the Mathematical Practices and ELA/literacy anchor standards?

   ☐ Not Yet   ☐ Some   ☐ Strong   ☐ Tight

6. Show other recommended improvements in instruction or content knowledge?

   ☐ Not Yet   ☐ Some   ☐ Strong   ☐ Tight

References and Resources

ACT. (2006). *Reading between the lines: What the ACT reveals about college readiness in reading.* Iowa City, IA: Author.

Afflerbach, P., Pearson, P. D., & Paris, S. G. (2008). Clarifying the differences between reading skills and reading strategies. *The Reading Teacher, 61*(5), 364–373.

Allington, R. L. (2011). What at-risk readers need. *Educational Leadership, 68*(6), 40–45.

Anderson, R. C. (1977). The notion of schemata and the educational enterprise: General discussion of the conference. In R. C. Anderson, R. J. Spiro, & W. W. Montague (Eds.), *Schooling and the acquisition of knowledge* (pp. 415–431). Mahwah, NJ: Erlbaum.

Atkin, J. (2011). *South Australian teaching for effective learning resource.* Adelaide, Australia: Government of South Australia, Department of Education and Children's Services.

Atkin, J., Barratt, R., Dutton, S., Foster, M., Green, C., Leaker, J., et al. (2010). *South Australian teaching for effective learning framework guide: A resource for developing quality teaching and learning in South Australia.* Adelaide, Australia: Government of South Australia, Department of Education and Children's Services. Accessed at www.learningtolearn.sa.edu.au/tfel/files/links/DECS_SA_TfEL_Framework_gu _3.pdf on January 23, 2013.

Barber, M., & Mourshed, M. (2007). *How the world's best-performing school systems come out on top.* Accessed at http://mckinseyonsociety.com/downloads/reports /Education/Worlds_School_Systems_Final.pdf on April 7, 2013.

Bellanca, J. A. (2010). *Enriched learning projects: A practical pathway to 21st century skills.* Bloomington, IN: Solution Tree Press.

Bellanca, J. A. (2012). *Projects from a box.* Glencoe, IL: International Renewal Institute.

Bellanca, J. A. (2013). *The focus factor.* New York: Teachers College Press.

Bellanca, J. A., & Brandt, R. (Eds.) (2010). *21st century skills: Rethinking how students learn.* Bloomington, IN: Solution Tree Press.

Bellanca, J., Fogarty, R., & Pete, B. (2012). *How to teach thinking skills within the Common Core: 7 key student proficiencies of the new national standards.* Bloomington, IN: Solution Tree Press.

Ben-Hur, M. (2006). *Concept-rich mathematics instruction: Building a strong foundation for reasoning and problem solving.* Alexandria, VA: Association for Supervision and Curriculum Development.

Bloom, B. (1984). *Taxonomy of educational objectives: Book 1:—Cognitive domain.* New York: Longman.

Bransford, J. D., Brown, A. I., & Cocking, R. R. (Eds.). (2000). *How people learn: Brain, mind, experience, and school.* Washington, DC: National Academies Press.

Brenner, D., & Hiebert, E. H. (2010). If I follow the teachers' editions, isn't that enough? Analyzing reading volume in six core programs. *Elementary School Journal, 110*(3), 347–363.

Brophy, J. E. (2006). Observational research on generic aspects of classroom teaching. In P. A. Alexander & P. H. Winne (Eds.), *Handbook of educational psychology* (pp. 755–780). Mahwah, NJ: Erlbaum.

Brophy, J. E., & Good, T. (1986). Teacher behavior and student achievement. In M. Wittrock (Ed.), *Third handbook of research on teaching* (pp. 328–375). Chicago: McNally.

Brummitt-Yale, J. (2008). *Boys and reading: Strategies for success.* Accessed at www.k12 reader.com/boys-and-reading on December 4, 2012.

Carroll, L. (1950). *Alice's adventures in Wonderland.* Chicago: McNally.

Carson, B. H. (1996). Thirty years of stories: The professor's place in student memories. *Change, 28*(6), 10–17.

Chetty, R., Friedman, J. N., & Rockoff, J. E. (2011). *The long-term impacts of teachers: Teacher value-added and student outcomes in adulthood.* Cambridge, MA: National Bureau of Economic Research. Accessed at http://obs.rc.fas.harvard.edu/chetty /value_added.pdf on June 12, 2012.

Cole, M. (Ed.). (1978). *Mind in society: The development of higher psychological processes.* Cambridge, MA: Harvard University Press.

Davidson, C. N. (2011). *Now you see it: How the brain science of attention will transform the way we live, work, and learn.* New York: Viking Press.

Deming, W. E. (1982). *Quality, productivity, and competitive position.* Cambridge, England: Massachusetts Institute of Technology, Center for Advanced Engineering Study.

Deming, W. E. (2000). *The new economics for industry, government, education* (2nd ed.). Cambridge, MA: MIT Press.

Denver Public Schools. (2011). *Secondary Literacy Standards Institute: Standards teacher leaders—June 2011, day one.* Accessed at http://curriculum.dpsk12.org /standards_implementation/June_2012_SecLit_Standards_Institute.pdf on January 23, 2013.

Dewey, J. (1938). *Experience and education.* New York: Macmillan.

Drago-Severson, E. (2009). *Leading adult learning: Supporting adult development in our schools.* Thousand Oaks, CA: Corwin Press.

DuFour, R. (2004). What is a professional learning community? *Educational Leadership, 61*(8), 6–11.

DuFour, R., DuFour, R., & Eaker, R. (2008). *Revisiting professional learning communities at work: New insights for improving schools.* Bloomington, IN: Solution Tree Press.

DuFour, R., DuFour, R., Eaker, R., & Many, T. (2010). *Learning by doing: A handbook for professional learning communities at work* (2nd ed.). Bloomington, IN: Solution Tree Press.

DuFour, R., & Eaker, R. (1998). *Professional learning communities at work: Best practices for enhancing student achievement.* Bloomington, IN: Solution Tree Press.

Fillmore, L. W. (2010). *Common Core standards: Can English learners meet them?* Paper presented at the English Language Learners Conference of the Council of Chief State School Officers, Alexandria, VA. Accessed at http://programs.ccsso.org /projects/ELLCONF/Presentations/Lily%20wong%20fillmore.pdf on January 23, 2013.

Fisher, D., & Frey, N. (2007). Implementing a schoolwide literacy framework: Improving achievement in an urban elementary school. *The Reading Teacher, 61*(1), 32–43.

Fogarty, R. (1997). *Problem-based learning and other curriculum models for the multiple intelligences classroom.* Arlington Heights, IL: IRI/Skylight Training.

Fogarty, R. (1998). *Balanced assessment.* Arlington Heights, IL: IRI/Skylight Training.

Fogarty, R., & Pete, B. (2007). *From staff room to classroom: A guide for planning and coaching professional development.* Thousand Oaks, CA: Corwin Press.

Fogarty, R., & Pete, B. (2011). *Supporting differentiated instruction: A professional learning communities approach.* Bloomington, IN: Solution Tree Press.

Fullan, M. G. (2001). *The new meaning of educational change* (3rd ed.). New York: Teachers College Press.

Gardner, M. (1941). The dinner party. *The Saturday Review of Literature, 25*(5).

George Lucas Educational Foundation. (2001, October 1). *From worms to Wall Street: Projects prompt active, authentic learning* [Video file]. Accessed at www.edutopia .org/newsome-park-elementary-project-learning-video on December 4, 2012.

Good, T. (2010). Forty years of research on teaching 1968–2008: What do we know now that we didn't know then? In R. J. Marzano (Ed.), *On excellence in teaching* (pp. 31–62). Bloomington, IN: Solution Tree Press.

Hall, S. L., & Moats, L. C. (1999). *Straight talk about reading: How parents can make a difference during the early years.* Lincolnwood, IL: Contemporary Books.

Hanushek, E. A., & Woessman, L. (2009). *Do better schools lead to more growth? Cognitive skills, economic outcomes, and causation* (Working Paper No. 14633). Cambridge, MA: National Bureau of Economic Research. Accessed at www.nber.org/papers/w14633.pdf on November 28, 2012.

Hattie, J. C. (2009). *Visible learning: A synthesis of over 800 meta-analyses relating to achievement.* New York: Routledge.

Hechinger Institute on Education and the Media. (n.d.). *Understanding and reporting on academic rigor: A Hechinger Institute primer for journalists.* New York: Author. Accessed at www.lrdc.pitt.edu/pubs/Abstracts/FiezRigorous.pdf on January 23, 2013.

Hewlett Foundation. (n.d.). *Deeper learning.* Accessed at www.hewlett.org/deeperlearning on May 12, 2012.

Hunter, M., & Russell, D. (1994). Planning for effective instruction: Lesson design. In M. Hunter (Ed.), *Enhancing teaching* (pp. 87–95). New York: Macmillan College.

Ishikawa, K. (1985). *What is total quality control? The Japanese way.* (D. J. Lu, Trans.) Englewood Cliffs, NJ: Prentice-Hall.

Jensen, L. (2009). *Explicit instruction.* Clearwater, KS: Service Center at ClearWater, South Central Kansas Education Service Center.

Joyce, B., & Showers, B. (1980). Improving inservice training: The messages of research. *Educational Leadership, 37*(5), 379–385.

Joyce, B., & Showers, B. (1983). *Power in staff development through research on training.* Alexandria, VA: Association for Supervision and Curriculum Development.

Joyce, B., & Showers, B. (1995). *Student achievement through staff development: Fundamentals of school renewal.* New York: Longman.

Joyce, B., & Showers, B. (2002). *Student achievement through staff development* (3rd ed.). Alexandria, VA: Association for Supervision and Curriculum Development.

Khan, U. (2009, April 3). *Leonardo da Vinci theme park to open in France.* Accessed at www.telegraph.co.uk/news/uknews/5098814/Leonardo-Da-Vinci-theme-park-to-open-in-France.html on May 10, 2012.

Killion, J. (2012). *Meet the promise of content standards: The principal.* Oxford, OH: Learning Forward. Accessed at www.learningforward.org/docs/commoncore/meetpromiseprincipal.pdf?sfvrsn=2 on January 2, 2013.

Knight, J. (2007). *Instructional coaching: A partnership approach to improving instruction.* Thousand Oaks, CA: Corwin Press.

Knowles, M. S. (1973). *The adult learner: A neglected species.* Houston, TX: Gulf.

Knowles, M., Holton, E. F., III, & Swanson, R. A. (2005). *The adult learner: The definitive classic in adult education and human resource development* (6th ed.). Burlington, MA: Elsevier.

Lobel, A. (1972). *Frog and toad together.* New York: HarperTrophy.

Maiers, A. (2009). *Recipe for learning success: I do, we do, you do.* Accessed at www.angelamaiers.com/2009/09/recipe-for-learning-success-i-do-you-do-we-do.html on November 29, 2012.

Marzano Research Laboratory. (2009a). *Instructional strategies.* Accessed at http://marzanoresearch.com/products/catalog.aspx?keywords=Instructional%20strategies on May 12, 2012.

Marzano Research Laboratory. (2009b). The *Marzano Common Core implementation.* Accessed at http://marzanoresearch.com/services/ccss.aspx on January 23, 2013.

Marzano Research Laboratory. (2009c). *Researched strategies.* Accessed at http://marzanoresearch.com/research/researched_strategies.aspx on June 1, 2012.

Masiello, R. (n.d.). *Teaching the academic language of close reading and quote analysis.* Boston: Houghton Mifflin. Accessed at www.docstoc.com/docs/17909682/Regina-Masiello on June 5, 2013.

Metiri Group. (2008). *Multimodal learning through media: What the research says.* Accessed at www.cisco.com/web/strategy/docs/education/Multimodal-Learning-Through-Media.pdf on May 12, 2012.

Monk, L. R. (2003). *The words we live by: Your annotated guide to the Constitution.* New York: Hyperion.

Mullis, I. V. S., Martin, M. O., Foy, P., & Drucker, K. T. (2012). *PIRLS 2011 international results in reading.* Chestnut Hill, MA: TIMSS & PIRLS International Study Center, Boston College. Accessed at http://timssandpirls.bc.edu/pirls2011/international-results-pirls.html on January 23, 2013.

National Council of Teachers of Mathematics. (2013). *Illuminations.* Accessed at http://illuminations.nctm.org on December 10, 2012.

National Governors Association Center for Best Practices & Council of Chief State School Officers. (2010a). *Common Core State Standards.* Washington, DC: Authors. Accessed at www.corestandards.org/the-standards on November 28, 2012.

National Governors Association Center for Best Practices & Council of Chief State School Officers. (2010b). *Common Core State Standards for English language arts & literacy in history/social studies, science, and technical subjects.* Washington, DC: Authors. Accessed at www.corestandards.org/ELA-Literacy on December 3, 2012.

National Governors Association Center for Best Practices & Council of Chief State School Officers. (2010c). *Common Core State Standards for English language arts & literacy in history/social studies, science, and technical subjects: Appendix A—Research supporting key elements of the standards.* Washington, DC: Authors. Accessed at www.corestandards.org/assets/Appendix_A.pdf on December 3, 2012.

National Governors Association Center for Best Practices & Council of Chief State School Officers. (2010d). *Common Core State Standards for English language arts & literacy in history/social studies, science, and technical subjects: Appendix B—Text exemplars and sample performance tasks.* Washington, DC: Authors. Accessed at www.corestandards.org/assets/Appendix_B.pdf on December 3, 2012.

National Governors Association Center for Best Practices & Council of Chief State School Officers. (2010e). *Common Core State Standards for mathematics.* Washington, DC: Authors. Accessed at www.corestandards.org/assets/CCSSI _Math%20Standards.pdf on May 10, 2012.

New Jersey Department of Education, (2004). *New Jersey core curriculum content standards.* Trenton, NJ: Author. Accessed at www.nj.gov/education/cccs/2004 /s3_lal.pdf on June 6, 2013.

Northwest Evaluation Association. (2012). *For every child, multiple measures: What parents and educators want from K–12 assessments.* Portland, OR: Author. Accessed at www.nwea.org/our-research/research-study-every-child-multiple-measures on January 9, 2013.

O'Connor, S. D. (2013). *Not your grandmother's civics: A conversation with Justice Sandra Day O'Connor.* Session presented at the Annual Conference of the Association for Supervision and Curriculum Development, Chicago, IL.

Organisation for Economic Co-operation and Development. (2009). *PISA 2009 key findings.* Paris: Author. Accessed at www.oecd.org/pisa/pisaproducts/pisa2009 /pisa2009keyfindings.htm on December 15, 2012.

Organisation for Economic Co-operation and Development. (2010a). *PISA 2012 mathematics framework.* Paris: Author. Accessed at www.oecd.org/pisa/pisa products/46961598.pdf on December 20, 2012.

Organisation for Economic Co-operation and Development. (2010b). *PISA 2012 field trial problem solving framework.* Paris: Author. Accessed at www.oecd.org/pisa /pisaproducts/46962005.pdf on May 12, 2012.

Parnes, S. J., Noller, R. B., & Biondi, A. M. (1977). *Guide to creative action.* New York: Scribner.

Partnership for 21st Century Skills. (2011). *Framework for 21st century learning.* Accessed at www.p21.org/overview/skills-framework on June 6, 2013.

Paul, R., & Elder, L. (2006). *The thinker's guide to how to read a paragraph and beyond: The art of close reading.* Tomales, CA: Foundation for Critical Thinking.

Pellegrino, J. W., & Hilton, M. L. (Eds.). (2012). *Education for life and work: Developing transferable knowledge and skills in the 21st century.* Washington, DC: National Academies Press.

Perkins, D., & Salomon, G. (1987). Transfer and teaching thinking. In D. N. Perkins, J. Lochhead, & J. Bishop (Eds.), *Thinking: The second international conference* (pp. 285–303). Hillsdale, NJ: Erlbaum.

Pete, B. M., & Fogarty, R. J. (2010). *From staff room to classroom II: The one-minute professional development planner.* Thousand Oaks, CA: Corwin Press.

Petry, A. (2001). *Harriet Tubman: Conductor on the Underground Railroad.* Logan, IA: Perfection Learning.

Piaget, J. (2011). *The language and thought of the child.* (Gabain & Gabain, Trans.). London: Routledge (Original work published 1926).

Piercy, T. (2011). *How close reading increases student access into complex text as expected in the ELA Common Core State Standards.* Englewood, CO: The Leadership and Learning Center.

Price, J., & Koretz, D. M. (2005). Building assessment literacy. In K. P. Boudett, E. A. City, & R. J. Murnane (Eds.), *Data wise: A step-by-step guide to using assessment results to improve teaching and learning* (pp. 29–55). Cambridge, MA: Harvard Education Press.

Quote Garden. (2011). *Quotations about math.* Accessed at ww.quotegarden.com/math .html on November 30, 2012.

Ravitz, J. (2009). Introduction: Summarizing findings and looking ahead to a new generation of PBL research. *Interdisciplinary Journal of Problem-Based Learning, 3*(1), 4–11. Accessed at http://docs.lib.purdue.edu/cgi/viewcontent.cgi?article=1088 &context=ijpbl on November 29, 2012.

Ronan, C. A. (2010). Telescopes. In *The New Book of Knowledge.* New York: Scholastic.

Simon, S. (2006). *Volcanoes.* New York: HarperCollins.

Sousa, D. A. (Ed.). (2010). *Mind, brain, & education: Neuroscience implications for the classroom.* Bloomington, IN: Solution Tree Press.

Southern Methodist University. (n.d.). *The unspoken speech: Text—Remarks prepared for delivery at the Dallas Trade Mart by President John F. Kennedy, November 22, 1963.* Accessed at http://smu.edu/smunews/jfk/speechtext.asp on January 23, 2013.

Stevens, J. (1995). *Tops and bottoms.* San Diego: Houghton Mifflin Harcourt.

Stiggins, R. J. (2002). Assessment crisis: The absence of assessment *for* learning. *Phi Delta Kappan*, *83*(10), 758–765.

TED. (2011, March). *Salman Khan: Let's use video to reinvent education* [Video file]. Accessed at www.ted.com/talks/salman_khan_let_s_use_video_to_reinvent _education.html on November 29, 2012.

Thayer, E. L. (1997) *Casey at the bat*. New York: Puffin.

University of Colorado at Boulder. (2011). *PhET: Interactive simulations*. Accessed at http://phet.colorado.edu on December 10, 2012.

U.S. Const. amend. I.

U.S. Const. pmbl.

von Frank, V. (2013). The power of observation: 5 ways to ensure teacher evaluations lead to teacher growth. *The Learning Principal*, *8*(2), 1, 4–5.

Weingarten, R. (2011). *Toward a true development and evaluation systems*. Accessed at www.aft.org/pdfs/press/sp_weingarten022411.pdf on April 19, 2013.

Wheatley, M. J. (2006). *Leadership and the new science: Discovering order in a chaotic world* (3rd ed.). San Francisco: Berrett-Koehler.

Yep, L. (1977). *Dragonwings*. New York: HarperCollins.

Index

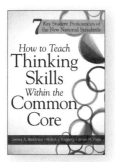

How to Teach Thinking Skills Within the Common Core
James A. Bellanca, Robin J. Fogarty, and Brian M. Pete
Empower your students to thrive across the curriculum. Packed with examples and tools, this practical guide prepares teachers across all grade levels and content areas to teach the most critical cognitive skills from the Common Core State Standards.
BKF576

Common Core English Language Arts in a PLC at Work™, Leader's Guide
Douglas Fisher, Nancy Frey, and Cynthia L. Uline
Integrate the CCSS for English language arts into your school's instruction, curriculum, assessment, and intervention practices with this straightforward resource. Using specific leader-driven examples and scenarios, discover the what and how of teaching so you can ensure students master the standards.
BKF578

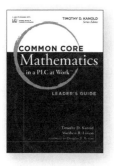

Common Core Mathematics in a PLC at Work™, Leader's Guide
Timothy D. Kanold and Matthew R. Larson
This leader companion to the teacher guides illustrates how to sustain successful implementation of the Common Core State Standards for mathematics. Comprehensive research-affirmed strategies will help collaborative teams develop and assess student demonstrations of deep conceptual understanding and procedural fluency.
BKF559

21st Century Skills
Edited by James A. Bellanca and Ron Brandt
Examine the Framework for 21st Century Learning from the Partnership for 21st Century Skills as a way to re-envision learning in a rapidly evolving global and technological world. Learn why these skills are necessary, which are most important, and how to best help schools include them.
BKF389

Wait! Your professional development journey doesn't have to end with the last pages of this book.

We realize improving student learning doesn't happen overnight. And your school or district shouldn't be left to puzzle out all the details of this process alone.

No matter where you are on the journey, we're committed to helping you get to the next stage.

Take advantage of everything from **custom workshops** to **keynote presentations** and **interactive web and video conferencing**. We can even help you develop an action plan tailored to fit your specific needs.

Let's get the conversation started.

Call 888.763.9045 today.

 solution-tree.com